GABRIEL MARCEL
THE DRAMATIST

Gabriel Marcel
the Dramatist

Hilda Lazaron

COLIN SMYTHE
GERRARDS CROSS, 1978

ISBN 0-901072-77-X

Distributed in North America by
Humanities Press, Inc., 171 First Avenue,
Atlantic Highlands, N.J. 07716.

Produced in Great Britain
by Billing & Sons Limited, Guildford,
London and Worcester

Preface

Gabriel Marcel the dramatist is not widely known in the United States even among those whose particular interest is the theatre. His philosophical works are well-known here, and his weekly reviews of the current Paris theatre are familiar to all readers of *Les Nouvelles Littéraires*. He has been a frequent lecturer on the Continent and in England; several of his plays including his two latest ones have been broadcast by the British Broadcasting Corporation.

Even in his native France, the plays of Gabriel Marcel have not met with the popular success on the stage that the importance of the work merits. Though he has a large reading public, only seven of his twenty published plays have been produced.

It is my good fortune to know Mr. Marcel personally. We met in 1951 and again in 1953, when he was recuperating from a serious automobile accident from which he has never completely recovered. He still walks with difficulty.

In 1955 when I spent the year in Paris, Mr. Marcel invited me to join a small discussion group which met in his apartment on the Rue de Tournon every Friday·afternoon from November to May. The group was composed of students, teachers and writers from many countries as well as from France, and the subjects discussed were unprepared and of wide diversity. Mr. Marcel acted more as participant than leader, in fact he was more silent than most of the group, always keenly interested in whatever contribution any member had to make. His sense of humor, his engaging warmth and kindness, made these sessions an unforgettable experience.

Most of the members of the group were students of philosophy. A few who were doing work on Mr. Marcel's theatre were making the study chiefly in an endeavour to link the plays with his philosophical works. Mr. Marcel frequently impressed upon the group his desire that his dramatic work not be considered a vehicle for the expression of his philosophical ideas. Since I wished to write about the plays for their own sake, this statement on his own position gave me great encouragement. The fact that he readily discussed the plays with me has been of inestimable help in the preparation of this analysis.

Many books, important articles and reviews have been written about Marcel's dramatic works during the last quarter century. These have contributed to our knowledge of Marcel as a dramatist. Among the more important of the lengthier works are a book by Joseph Chenu,[1] a symposium edited by Etienne Gilson,[2] and an essay of Roger Troisfontaines.[3] These, while stressing the importance of Marcel as a dramatist, fail to consider the plays solely as drama. These studies consider the plays primarily as illustrations of Marcel's philosophical ideas and seek to find analogies between the plays and the philosophy.

The numerous individual articles and reviews which have appeared in many languages have shed important light on Marcel's plays, but all of these together could not possibly constitute a complete study of this theatre, nor any analysis of the parallel developments in Marcel's life and his drama.

There is still room, consequently, for a study of all the plays completely divorced from the philosophical work. Such a study must present the plays in great detail because of the general lack of familiarity with them.

This study begins with Marcel's biography (Chapter I), and what can be considered the keynote of his dramatic work (Chapter II). The long Chapter III contains twenty plays. Here the plays are treated as the expression of Marcel's own experience and the reflection of the times in which they were often written. Chronological order has been sacrificed in favor of a grouping according to subject matter, although frequently chronology and subject matter coincide. Group 1 contains Marcel's first two plays and two other written some ten years later. They are considered together because of their relatively abstract nature, which is not characteristic of the other plays. Group 2 contains four plays in which the action takes place during or immediately following World War I. In Group 3 there are six plays which cover a period from 1921 to 1938; they are concerned solely with personal and family relationships and tensions. The theme of Group 4 is World War II and the order happens to be chronological. The subject is the effect of the war on various groups in France. The last two plays, (Group 5) that I deal with, were published in 1955, and deal with contemporary problems.

Chapter IV attempts to place Marcel the dramatist among his contemporaries; and the Appendix contains a short summary of the five plays in his so-called "comic theatre".

A word should be said here about the general character of the plays. Marcel refuses to accept the label "thesis" or "problem" as applied to his plays. He differentiates between the problems in a social theatre which he calls external and for which there is some solution, and the problems in his own drama which are psychological. He declares that the characters of Brieux, Sartre and others which are created solely by the authors to express their own point of view differ from his characters which have a life and will of their own. Marcel prefers to call his plays "plays or ideas" in which the development of character and conflict of personality are the chief purpose. He claims that a predominance of ideas does not necessarily cause a play to be either a "thesis" or a "problem" play if the development of character is the final objective.

NOTES

[1] Joseph Chenu, *Le Théâtre de Gabriel Marcel et sa signification métaphysique*, Aubier, 1948.

[2] J. P. Dubois-Dumée, "Solitude et Communion dans le théâtre de Gabriel Marcel", *Existentialisme Chrétien*, présentation de Etienne Gilson, Paris, Plon, 1947.

[3] Roger Troisfontaines, "De l'existence à l'être", Paris, Editions J. Vrin, 1953. 2 V.

Contents

Part Three

Part One

CHAPTER I

Gabriel Marcel, the Man

Doubtless because of Gabriel Marcel's extraordinary reticence about himself, few biographical details concerning him have been published. The only direct source is the essay entitled "Regard en arrière" which he contributed to the symposium edited by Etienne Gilson, *L'Existentialisme chrétien*.[1] There, in a searching backward glance, he attempts to disengage the significance of his early life, believing that the spiritual repercussions of the mere facts outweigh the facts themselves.

Thus we know that he was born in Paris on December 7, 1889, of intellectual parents. His father, Henri Camille, Marcel (1854–1926), Conseiller d'Etat, was the author of numerous studies in the history of art, particularly in the field of nineteenth century French painting.[2] His mother, Laure Meyer, was of Jewish parentage but not affiliated with any church. She died suddenly when her only child was but four years old. Hence little Gabriel was brought up by her sister, who became the second Mme Henri Marcel. Such are the bare facts, but their implications for Gabriel Marcel are of great importance for an understanding of his creative work:

Mais songez que toute mon enfance, que vraisemblablement ma vie entière a été dominée par la mort de ma mère, mort absolument soudaine qui devait bouleverser toutes nos existences. C'était, d'après ce qui m'a été dit d'elle, et autant que j'ai pu en juger par des lettres étincelantes, un être exceptionnel et merveilleusement accordé à la vie. Mon père, qui se reprocha, je crois, de lui avoir imposé d'excessives fatigues soit en voyage soit dans la campagne électorale qu'il fit avec elle dans les Basses-Alpes au printemps de 1893, avait trouvé en elle une compagne incomparable qui s'associait de toute son ardeur à ses goûts, á ses curiosités. Je l'ai dit j'allais avoir quatre ans quand je la perdis. Indépendamment des rares images précises que j'ai pu conserver d'elle, elle m'est restée présente, mystérieusement elle a toujours été avec moi. Mais cependant ma tante, aussi douée peût-étre, mais très différente, devait inévitablement l'éclipser en fait, et je crois comprendre aujourd'hui que cette étrange dualité au coeur de ma vie entre un être disparu dont par pudeur ou par désespoir on parlait assez rarement, et sur lequel une sorte de crainte révérentielle me retenait de poser des questions,—et un autre être, extraordinairement affirmé, dominateur, et qui se croyait tenu de projeter la lumière dans les moindres encoignures de mon existence,—je soupçonne, dis-je, que cette disparité, ou cette polarité secrète de l'invisible et du visible, a exercé sur ma pensée, et bien au delà de ma pensée exprimée, sur mon être même, une influence occulte qui a dépassé infiniment toutes celles dont mes écrits presentent des traces discernables.

Mon enfance, dis-je, a souffert d'un état d'hypertension, et comme de harcèlement intérieur qui à certaines époques atteignit un paroxysme intolérable. Je souffrais de la façon la plus consciente et parfois la plus aigüe de sentir qu'étant enfant unique, je comptais trop pour les miens, tout ce qui me touchait avait trop d'importance, mes indispositions comme mes succès ou mes échecs scolaires. Je me sentais continuellement surveillé, épié, je devinais que lorsque j'étais allé me coucher on s'interrogeait sur moi, sur mes insuffisances, sur ce qu'on pouvait ou non raisonnablement attendre de moi. Notre absurde système scolaire, qui pour n'être pas entièrement nocif, devrait comporter comme contre-partie chez les parents une certaine dose d'indifférence et de scepticisme, exerça au contraire à plein dans mon cas ses effets maléfiques.

Mes parents avaient été des élèves extrêmement brillants. Aussi attachaient-ils à mes notes, à mes places une importance démesurée. Dans ces conditions, chaque composition devenait un drame; je croyais sentir que c'était au fond chaque fois pour les miens une occasion de me remettre en question—puisqu'on ne semblait guère distinguer entre moi et mon rendement scolaire. Certes, j'exprime cela aujourd'hui en un langage que je n'aurais pas eu alors á ma disposition, mais je suis tout à fait sûr que cette crainte, cette angoisse est à l'origine du souvenir détestable que j'ai gardé de mes années de lycée, et aussi du jugement que je porte encore à présent sur un régime scolaire qui pèche par une méconnaissance radicale de la réalité et surtout du mode de croissances des êtres; aussi, bien que j'aie été ce qu'on appelle "un excellent élève," que j'aie obtenu á peu près tous les prix de le cinquième à la philosophie, je n'hésite pas à penser que ces années ont correspondu pour moi à un véritable arrêt de développement sur le plan intellectuel, et que physiquement elles ont contribué à me faire la médiocre santé qui a été la mienne depuis cette époque.[3]

The *lycée* that Marcel attended was the Lycée Carnot in Paris, which he entered in 1899 at the age of ten. But before starting that formal schooling, he spent several months in Stockholm, where his parents took him in his ninth year. Looking back in later life, he saw that period of freedom as a sharp contrast to the ensuing school years:

A Stockholm, ce paysage de rochers, d'arbres et d'eau, dont je devais garder pendant des années la nostalgie, dut, j'imagine, m'apparaître comme celui qui symbolisait le mieux l'univers douloureux que je portais en moi. Cette nostalgie s'explique cependant aussi par le fait que, pendant l'année que nous passâmes en Suède, toute fréquentation scolaire me fut épargnée, et que j'éprouvai d'autre part un certain plaisir à me lier avec les autres enfants du corps diplomatique, et à entrevoir derrière chacun d'eux un monde étrange et attirant. Je me trouvai ainsi élevé à la fois à la maison, au sein des miens—et tout de même mis en contact avec un monde infiniment divers au devant duquel me portait ma passion spontanée pour les voyages et pour la géographie. Le lycée où j'entrai dix-huit mois après notre retour de Suède formait un contraste qui me parut meurtrissant avec la vie libre, personnelle, ouverte sur l'inconnu, qui avait été la mienne à Stockholm ... Je suis tenté de me demander aujourd'hui si mon aversion pour le lycée n'est pas à l'origine de l'horreur croissante que devait m'inspirer l'esprit d'abstraction dont ce même lycée était après tout le dérisoire palladium.[4]

In his "Regard en arrière" Gabriel Marcel, in fact, expatiates on the "régime abstrait et inhumain du lycée" which disgusted him with most of the literature he was forced to analyse in class. But he was also a prey at the same time to a certain vague anguish that went beyond the arid impressions communicated by school:

Il est clair à mes yeux, lorsque je considère aujourd'hui les années difficiles qui précédèrent mon initiation philosophique, que l'angoisse continuelle qui était liée pour moi à la vie scolaire s'articulait avec un sentiment informulé de l'irrévocable et de la mort. Comment au surplus pourrais-je expliquer autrement l'espèce de terreur qui s'emparait de moi le nuit lorsque mes parents tardaient à rentrer après un dîner ou un spectacle?[5]

Despite such emotional difficulties, however, the boy consistently remained one of the best pupils in his class. Upon graduation from the *lycée*, he entered the Sorbonne and passed the difficult Agrégation de Philosophie in 1909. For the next thirty years, then, he was to teach philosophy classes in various *lycées*, starting at Vendôme and moving to Sens, Paris, and Montpellier. The two most distinguished schools in which he taught were both in Paris: the Lycée Condorcet (1915-18) and the Lycée Louis Le Grand (1939-40).

It was during the years immediately preceding the first World War that Gabriel Marcel's reflections on metaphysics led him to his "premiers énoncés existentialistes". Despite whatever premonitions he may have had of the approaching catastrophe, especially after the Agadir crisis, he did not suspect, he says, the fragility of the civilization to which centuries had given a kind of unquestioned solidity:

Certes à distance, les contours se simplifient à l'excès, mais il me semble bien, en ce qui me concerne, que l'illusion dans laquelle nous vivions à le veille du cataclysme m'a seule permis d'accomplir la partie préliminaire, mais aussi la plus ardue de ma recherche. Le changement de ton ou de régistre qu'on note dans la deuxième partie du Journal s'explique presque complètement par l'ébranlement que me causa la guerre.[6]

The reference is to his *Journal métaphysique* which he began keeping in 1913 and did not publish until 1927. It is characteristic of the man that the only diary he has ever published should be qualified as "metaphysical" and be limited to a record of his intellectual and spiritual evolution.

Today Marcel wishes that his name and work could be divorced from the term "Existentialist" which he feels carries so much false connotation. In the Introduction to one of his philosophical works, *Le Mystère de l'être*, he protests against "les déplorables confusions auxquelles a donné lieu dans mon cas l'affreux vocable d'Existentialisme", adding that if he chose any *-ism* at all, it would be that of "néo-Socratisme" or "Socratisme chrétien".[7] Nonetheless, the label of "existentialisme chrétien" will in all probability remain attached to his name, as it is today in most manuals.

Gabriel Marcel does not ignore the Existentialist's "angoisses", especially that which is provoked by the thought of death and the idea of life's absurdity. He also admits the impossibility of refuting the partisans of suicide. The consent to live is an affair of free-will and an act of faith; it is only by making this option that he escapes the pessimism of the atheistic Existentialist. As his plays show, the need to hope is basic in him. Hence the philosopher accepts the theory of the absurdity of existence but the injured spirit rejects the "néant".

Such a compromise reflects the philosopher's increasing sympathy for Christianity during these same years. The son of an agnostic father who had been nourished on Taine, Spencer, and Renan and of a mother completely detached from all religious belief or practice, he had neither been baptized nor received any form of religious training. His mother's early death naturally raised questions in his young mind; yet he was not aware, during his schooldays, of suffering from the lack of a faith. Indeed, he notes:

Mais élevé en dehors de toute foi et de toute pratique je ne pense pas avoir jamais envié, lorsque j'étais enfant, ceux de mes camarades qui recevaient un enseignement confessionnel: il est vrai que mes amis appartenaient eux aussi à des familles incroyantes; sur les bancs du lycée où j'étais externe, je coudoyais des garçons qui venaient d'institutions religieuses, mais je suis à peu près sûr de n'avoir jamais arrêté ma pensée sur la nourriture spirituelle qu'ils pouvaient y puiser; ou plus exactement, j'inclinais me semble-t-il à croire cette nourriture inexistante. Au fond, j'admettais confusément à cette époque que, de nos jours, un homme intelligent peut encore à la rigueur être un protestant, parce que le protestantisme comporte le libre examen, mais qu'en revanche, on ne peut demeurer catholique qu'à la faveur de beaucoup de sottise et d'une profonde hypocrisie. Je ne saurais donc prétendre avoir comme enfant la nostalgie des biens qui m'étaient refusés.[8]

His philosophical speculations, however, though starting from an inherited agnosticism, early reflected a deep spiritual need. Nothing in the "milieu" or family of Marcel explains his great interest in religion. In his doctoral thesis, never completed, he proposed to elucidate "à quelles conditions la pensée religieuse peut être pensée (c'est-à-dire intelligible)". The conversion of his close friend Charles du Bos did not influence him at this time. But from the time he commenced writing his *Journal métaphysique*, January 1, 1914, until its completion, in March 1923, he filled its pages with passages indicating his deep spiritual searching.

On February 1st, 1914,[9] he writes: "La conversion n'est pensable que par l'intervention de la Grâce. Mais la conversion est-elle pensable?" And on the same date,[10] "La question est donc de savoir comment la Grâce peut être pensée comme réelle, comment la pensée peut arriver à frapper d'invalidité l'acte par lequel elle prétendrait voir dans la Grâce l'expression illusoire, fixée, d'une activité qui ne parviendrait pas à être pour soi". February 3rd:[11] "Je raisonnerais en somme comme suit" si la conversion est possible, ce ne peut être que par l'intervention de la Grâce ... Il est absurde de se demander s'il est légitime de penser la Grâce, en ce que la Grâce doit par définition tomber en dehors des normes de la réflexion."[12] February 25, 1920,[13] "La volonté divine n'est elle qu'une fiction recouvrant les causes? ou bien est-elle une puissance? et dans ce cas ne restons-nous pas dans le pur causal?"

Certainly Marcel's philosophic origins, the influence of Husserl and Heidegger, of his old professor Brunschweig and the profound impression made on him by Bergson, as well as the influence of Jewry, are important in his spiritual anabasis. But from 1924 to 1929 he even abandoned philosophic research and it was not until February 25, 1929, following a review he wrote of Mauriac's *Dieu et Mannon*, having received a letter from Mauriac which ended with the words, "Mais enfin pourquoi n'êtes-vous pas des nôtres?", that Marcel decided to ask for baptism. On March 5, 1929,

Marcel wrote: "Je ne doute plus. Miraculeux bonheur, ce matin. J'ai fait pour la première fois clairement l'expérience de la Grâce. Ces mots sont effrayants, mais c'est cela. J'ai été enfin cerné par le christianisme, et je suis submergé. Et pourtant j'en ai comme le besoin. Impression de balbutiement ... C'est bien une naissance. Tout est autrement, je vois clair aussi, maintenant, dans mes improvisations. Une autre métaphore inverse de l'autre—celle d'un monde qui était là entièrement présent et qui affleure enfin."[14]

On March 23, 1929, at the age of 39 Gabriel Marcel was baptised in the Roman Catholic Church in a state of mind which he describes "une disposition intérieure que j'osais à peine espérer: aucune exaltation mais un sentiment de paix, d'équilibre, d'espérance, de foi".[15]

Gabriel Marcel began writing the plays we know as early as 1911, very soon after the end of his formal studies and the beginning of his career. His turning to drama as expression of his spiritual anxiety is incontestably revealed in his plays. But there were other motivations.

Si l'on songe que depuis mon enfance j'ai été hanté par le théâtre, conçu beaucoup moins comme un spectacle que comme un mode d'expression privilégié. Sans bien entendu que ma prédilection pour le dialogue fût alors en état de rendre compte d'elle-même, mon goût me portait naturellement non vers le récit ou vers la description, mais vers un art qui se dissimule en quelque sorte derrière les sujets qu'il confronte. Je l'ai dit ailleurs, j'ai ressenti de très bonne heure une sorte d'ivresse non seulement à évoquer des êtres distincts de moi, mais à m'identifier assez complètement à eux pour devenir leur truchement.

Il serait vain de se demander à quoi tint chez moi cette disposition. Le fait que mon père avait un sens inné du théâtre et était un lecteur de pièces incomparable n'est certainement pas négligeable. Mais j'ai toujours pensé que les personnages de théâtre que je me plaisais à faire dialoguer me tinrent lieu à l'origine des frères et soeurs dont je déplorais cruellement l'absence.

Une autre circonstance contribua sans doute au développement de mes facultés dramatiques. Je me trouvai appelé, dès mon enfance, à observer entre ceux qui composaient mon milieu familial des divergences de vues et de tempéraments qui me contraignirent a prendre prématurément conscience des "insolubilia" que comportent souvent les rapports humains en apparence les plus simples.[16]

The composition of Marcel's first two plays *La Grâce* and *Le Palais de sable* (in 1911) preceded the beginning of his *Metaphysical Journal* by three years. He says:

> ... ce que j'aperçois surtout aujourd'hui avec une très grande netteté c'est que le mode de penser dramatique, qui consiste à poser des sujets en tant que sujets, c'est-à-dire dans leur réalité de sujets, illustrait et justifiait à l'avance tout ce que j'ai pu écrire plus tard dans un régistre purement philosophique au sujet d'une connaissance qui transcende l'objectivité bien, loin de se confiner dans la sphère de la subjectivité immédiate. Je note seulement que ce rapprochement s'est effectué dans ma pensée à une époque relativement tardive, aux alentours de 1930. Pourquoi les deux modes d'expression qui étaient les miens se sont-ils ainsi développés de façon autonome et comme à l'écart l'un de l'autre. C'est là une question à laquelle il m'est assez difficile de répondre. Je suppose cependant que si une communication prématurée s'était établie entre eux, c'eût été aux dépens de ce que chacun d'eux avait en soi de vivace et d'authentique. Ce ne peut être un hasard, si celles de mes pièces qui m'apparaissent aujourd'hui les plus riches de substance spirituelle sont celles d'où toute préméditation philosophique est le plus manifestement absente.[17]

This statement should give pause, especially to those students of Marcel's philosophical works who conceive of his drama as merely an expression of his philosophical ideas. He has frequently called this notion completely false.[18], [19]

In the preface to *De l'Existence à l'être*[20] he says, "je suis loin au reste de penser que c'est à partir des oeuvres d'art que la vie doit être interprétée et je ne parle pas, bien entendu, de la vie comme phénomène naturel, mais de notre vie atteinte dans sa matière et dans son intimité".

Art in its various forms has been of supreme importance in moulding the life and thinking of Marcel. The music of Bach and, later, the picture of Giotto furnished him with spiritual nourishment. "Pour ce qui est de Bach, je crois bien l'avoir toujours connu et aimé ... au fond la vie chrétienne m'est venue à travers cela."[21]

Marcel's plays grow directly from his early formation,

particularly from the fact of his mother's early death and his being brought up as an only child by his step-mother—the same fact that presumably determined his metaphysical penchant and his eventual conversion to Catholicism.

"Il n'y a qu'une souffrance" says Rose, the heroine in *Le Coeur des autres*, one of Marcel's early plays, "il n'y a qu'une souffrance, c'est d'être seul", this statement is echoed by almost everyone of Marcel's protagonists and expresses one of his major themes. "Rien n'est jamais perdu pour un homme, s'il vit un grand amour ou une véritable amitié, mais tout est perdu pour celui qui est seul."[22]

In the twenty plays presented here, man is alone. Communion is made possible only through love. Beyond this there is the "mystère". "... il y a une valeur propre du mystère ... il y a certains rapports qui ne se définissent et ne s'élucident que par la communion dans le mystère".[23] Most of the characters seek clarity for themselves and relation with others through this "mystère". "... il y a une étroite interdépendance de nos destinées spirituelles."[24]

But there is still another step necessary for man to achieve his release from loneliness—pride must be replaced by humility—then hope become possible and hope is paramount in the majority of Marcel's plays. "... Malgré toutes les possibilités sinistres qui nous cernent, le dernier mot appartient à l'espérance, il n'en peut être ainsi que dans la mesure où je me suis trouvé personnellement incapable de coller a cette réalité technicisable ...: ... celle-ci ne peut pas plus donner lieu à l'espérance que l'asphalte d'un trottoir ne peut nourrir serait-ce un brin d'herbe."[25]

Marcel's need to hope is not only the mainspring of his dramatic work, it also prompted him to metaphysical speculation and was a significant influence toward his conversion. Maurice Martin de Gard, in an article following the publication in book form of *Le Regard neuf, Le Mort de demain* and *La Chapelle ardente* says: "Nous espérons que la conversion de Gabriel Marcel renouvellera son art dramatique, en l'affermissant, bien qu'il nous ait avoué jusqu'ici que son talent, comme la plupart des talents, du reste était surtout fait de son inquiétude ... il enrichit l'esprit plus qu'il ne l'excite, et rien n'est plus émouvant que sa nostalgie de l'authenticité quand il écrit aussi bien que dans sa conversation familière toujours obsédée par sa torture de tout préciser, jusqu'à Dieu lui-même."[26]

Had it not been for this "inquiétude" we should never have had the majority of these plays. The dialogue in his mind would have ceased. There is no possible suggestion of insincerity in Marcel's action but I believe that the plays demonstrate that his acceptance of dogmatic religion was never complete, and that the dualism in his soul is apparent to this day. He is forced to compromise with religion in the same manner as he had done previously with Existentialism. To the Existentialist he says, "I agree—but—"; and to Roman Catholicism he says, "I believe—but—". The *I believe* is the answer of his great concern over his soul and his salvation, of his loneliness and his need, along with his natural response to the artistic and the mystic in the Roman Catholic faith. And still the *but* remains. He has not found serenity. The plays are really Existentialist plays where Hope comes sometimes at the end of the journey, Hope and Faith.

But it may well be asked, if Faith and Hope can come at the end of the journey, does this not prove Marcel's acceptance and make valid his statement of belief. To this the answer is evident, particularly in the later plays. Marcel's revolt is against the uncritical acceptance of dogmatic theology. His is the struggle of the anti-conformist, of the individualist, against authority.

NOTES

[1] Etienne Gilson, *L'Existentialisme chrétien*, 1947, Paris, Plon, p. 291.
[2] His works include:
La Bibliothèque Nationale, 2 volumes, 1907
Honoré Daumier, Biographie Critique Illustré, 1906
J. F. Millet, Biographie Critique, 1909
Manuel d'histoire de l'art, 1904
La peinture française au XIX siècle, 1905
Introduction Biographique, *Théodore Chassériau* par Jean Laran, 1905.
[3] *L'Existentialisme chrétien*, p. 302.
[4] *Ibid.*, p. 303.
[5] *Ibid.*, p. 303.
[6] *Ibid.*, p. 311.
[7] *Le Mystère de l'être*, p. iii.
[8] "Regard en arrière", *L'Existentialisme chrétien*, p. 300.

[9] *Journal métaphysique*, p. 51.
[10] *Ibid.*, p. 54.
[11] *Ibid.*, p. 55.
[12] *Ibid.*, p. 55.
[13] *Ibid.*, p. 229.
[14] *Etre et avoir*, p. 17.
[15] *Ibid.*, p. 30.
[16] *Existentialisme chrétien*, p. 294.
[17] *Ibid.*, pp. 296 f.
[18] "Drama of the Soul in Exile", p. 33 (dissertation p. 10).
[19] *Existentialisme chrétien*, p. 212.
[20] P. ii.
[21] *Témoignage chrétien*, p. 48.
[22] Preface to *De l'Existence à l'être*, pp. 302 f.
[23] *Journal Métaphysique*, p. 159.
[24] *Etre et Avoir*, p. 26.
[25] Preface *De l'Existence à l'être*, p. iii.
[26] *Les Nouvelles Littéraires*, April 23, 1932.

CHAPTER II

The Drama of the Soul in Exile

In the preface to Roger Troisfontaine's *De l'Existence à l'être*[1] Gabriel Marcel writes: "Mon théâtre est le théâtre de l'âme en exil, de l'âme qui souffre du manque de communion avec elle-même et avec les autres. Le mensonge intérieur y joue un rôle prépondérant. L'âme en exil, c'est l'âme aliénée, devenue étrangère à elle-même, et pour elle-même à peu près incompréhensible. Thème général qui se diversifie à l'infini, mais culmine dans le voeu de Claude Lemoine à la fin de *Un Homme de Dieu*, 'Etre connu tel qu'on est.'"

Marcel again used the phrase "drama of the soul in exile" as the title for a lecture he gave in July 1950 at the Institut Français in London (published in London, 1952, by Secker and Warburg). Here Marcel proposed to throw light on what the theatre has never ceased to represent to him and to indicate the apparent general trend of his own plays, when considered chronologically. "That this title is open to serious misunderstanding, I fully realize, for the Platonists throughout the ages, the 'soul in exile' has always been the soul sunk, after some scarcely imaginable spiritual disaster, in the darkness of the world of sense, and aspiring to expand once more in some intelligible empyrean. It is more than evident that—this theme than which, perhaps, there is none less dramatic—is entirely absent from my work."[2]

The general theme of Marcel's drama is man's aloneness in the universe; he is a stranger to himself and incomprehensible to others. His misunderstanding of his own intentions and behavior spreads misery. Using one of his plays *La Chapelle ardente* to illustrate his point, Marcel describes its central theme as "a living relationship seen at work in a particular situation" and states that what he wanted to bring out in the last act is "the kind of fatality which a human being can carry in himself and constantly discharge upon others, even when his intentions are above reproach". Then Marcel states that often the most apparently conscious and clear-headed are most ignorant of their inner selves. In *La Chapelle ardente* the inner vision which the characters themselves lack, is transferred by the dramatist to the spectator who, through profound understanding becomes like a higher being. This transferral, he says, must be accomplished not on the abstract level, but on the level of action, without any decrease in the reality and individuality of the character.

At this point Marcel seeks to justify a realistic theatre and denies that the task necessitates a more courageous use of transposition and poetic style than his. He states that the playright must lead the spectator to the vital, focal point in himself, which is the ideal observation post. It is wrong to imagine that this need be done by the introduction of exterior or extra-human elements. If however the substance of drama is not an incarnation of thought, the plays become mere spectacle. Marcel states that the use of transposition and escape into a poetic and stylized world is less effective than the use of creatures whose problems resemble those of the spectator.

In speaking of his characters, Marcel explains the relation between a stage character and the person who has stimulated the author to conceive that character. The people in his plays have usually come into being as a result of a chance meeting which stimulated his curiosity. This imperfect and fragmentary experience sometimes resulted in the creation of a somewhat ambiguous character; but this seeming failure is often the proof of the dramatist's success as a creator. As an example of his uncertainty about a character which he himself had conceived, Marcel cites Ariane in *Le Chemin de Crête*. He says "while writing this play I had far less feeling of creation than of recognition. I found myself faced with a character so resistant and so distinct from myself, that I was forced to give up the ending I had planned because she rejected it. 'You can't do that with me' she said. 'If you insist I shall disappear.' But to the extent that this character resisted me, I am justified in saying that it contains an element which remains to me irreducible". In the theatre, Marcel says, effective magic can reach us only through the characters, and is induced by the manner in which they make their presence felt; felt more authentically even than that of our daily companions. Without such characters, the drama is no more than a trivial game of scenic effects and technical skill.

In many of Marcel's plays the dead play a part at least as active as the living. Their role is fundamental because it is accompanied by a deeper delving into their past lives. The destiny of these characters reveals itself, thus making the ending of a play its most important point. Marcel adds that the quality of a play can only be judged by its last act. This explanation removes from the realm of the strictly morbid Marcel's use of the dead as many of his chief characters.

While many of the plays close on a sombre note, from others there springs a flash of dazzling light at the end. Marcel calls this flash of light "illumination" and believes that the use of it is a most effective technique in the theatre, where truths which are demonstrable and susceptible to proof dare not have the freedom of the stage. He admits to sometimes pushing illumination too far, making the end of some of his plays too improbable. What he wishes to bring out is how the illumination "in itself a grace emanating from a sanctified personality can retrospectively throw light on the groping efforts of a character".

In Marcel's later plays the horizon widens. The basic theme now is the suffering of the contemporary world (*Le Dard, L'Emissaire, Le Signe de la croix, Rome n'est plus dans Rome*). These, however, are not works for a social theatre as it was conceived at the end of the nineteenth century by naturalistic writers, such as Brieux or even Gerhardt Hauptmann. Since the problems in Marcel's plays lie in the inner world of the human soul, the word problem can hardly be used; for where there cannot be a solution, there cannot in exact parlance be a problem. Marcel then states that here we are beyond all technique, and man, faced with an ever-deepening chasm, is left to his own resources so that an attempted solution is never more than a procedure invented by the human spirit to cope with a particular difficulty.

There is never any excuse says Marcel, for a playwright to climb into a pulpit. If he attempts to preach he betrays his mission. Also he must beware of prophetic consciousness, "for the vocation of the prophet is an exceptional one and can only be submitted to". Marcel says that philosophical drama "whose champion I, by some woeful misconception have at times been taken to be" has no more determined opponent than he.

Marcel states that the keynote of his dramatic work is ethical rather than religious. It is goodwill in the Gospel rather than the Kantian sense, the will to remain faithful "to an interior light which is too often intercepted by a coalition of powerful forces born of our own vanity". Life itself will confound the iconoclast ... life, or He who is beyond words.

Critics of Marcel's drama have sometimes recognized his fundamental objectives, and have acknowledged a measure of success in reaching them. Others are in sharp disagreement. Clouard in his *Histoire de la littérature française,*[3] states that philosophers suffer from being classified as "dialogueurs à thèses" and that the one who least deserves this characterization as a dramatist is Gabriel Marcel.

Gabriel Marcel met à la scène des décisions d'esprit, des attitudes de caractère et tout un tragique de la personne concrète, incarnée, celle dont il est le métaphysicien et dont il creuse la réalité jusqu'à en faire jaillir l'appel de l'homme à Dieu. Il montre des consciences déchirées: les unes violentes et absolues; les autres douces, complexes, toutes travaillées par les tentations de l'existence et par les offres de l'universelle contradiction. L'auteur ne les juge point, il les fait s'affronter pour découper en reliefs significatifs quelques grands aspects de la bataille éternelle de l'âme avec la chair, de l'amour avec l'égoïsme, de l'héroïsme avec toutes sortes d'inconscientes contraintes.

Clouard in these few lines points out many of the essentials of Marcel's drama, and by these examples shows clearly that they are not *pièces à thèses.*

Théâtre éminemment naturel. Ses personnages mènent leur

vie, les caractères s'installent chacun dans sa singularité, les fils se nouent, et des significations émergent spontanément, portées par une parole ou un geste, par un choc de répliques. Or nous n'en voyons pas moins se développer des expériences individuelles, familiales, sociales, et qui prétendent à une valeur métaphysique. Car ne rien perdre de son bagage de métaphysicien, rien d'essentiel en tenant néanmoins très solidement les planches, telle a été l'ambition de Gabriel Marcel. L'a-t-il réalisée?

Oui, par un effort d'idéalisme scrupuleux, quoique assez tard, il a fini par s'emparer d'un public resté longtemps réticent.

It must be admitted that, however successful Marcel has been in realizing his objectives dramatically, he still has a small and reticent public.

Marcel Doisy in *Le Théâtre français contemporain* finds that Marcel has succeeded in but few of his objectives. He says:

Gabriel Marcel procède à la fois d'Ibsen et du Théâtre-Libre, et les ambitions qui animent son oeuvre sont nobles. Il faut bien reconnaître cependant, malgré toute l'estime que commande un effort aussi désintéressé que le sien, qu'il ne parvient que rarement à communiquer un souffle de vie authentique à ses personnages. Encore une fois, il ne peut être question ici de théâtre à thèse au sens où le pratiquait Brieux, mais plutôt de théâtre à tendance où le penseur—voire même le croyant—prime l'artiste. Ce théâtre sévère et substantiel témoigne d'un idéalisme respectable que les esprits très chrétiens placeront sans doute assez haut, mais pour des raisons probablement étrangères à la pure esthétique. Son défaut essentiel est son inhumanité, se manifestant principalement dans la vie très artificielle des personnages. Contrairement à l'ordre naturel des choses qui voudrait que d'un conflit vivant surgissent des thèses de méditation, on voit ici des données intellectuelles imposées à des personnages vidés de substance physique et asservis au rôle de moyens d'expression.

Sa nature même condamnait d'avance cet austère écrivain à n'atteindre que des succès d'estime et il est peu probable qu'il conserve une place importante parmi les grands dramaturges de ce temps. Sans doute est-ce également au Théâtre d'idées que l'on doit rattacher, bien que dans un tout autre ordre, le théâtre tardivement conçu du romancier.

This criticism will certainly find opposition even from those who are not admirers of Marcel's work. The statement that "il ne parvient que rarement à communiquer un souffle de vie authentique à ses personnages" seems particularly harsh when considering the dramatic work as a whole. But more unjust still is the statement that his greatest fault is his inhumanity, expressed in the life of his characters seems even less penetrating.

M. Edmond Jaloux is more perceptive in his remarks which appeared in *Les Nouvelles Littéraires.*[4] Admitting that the acts of Marcel's heroes result from the patterns of their thinking, he makes the following statement:

> Chez M. Marcel nous voyons des personnages soumis à la fois à leurs réactions autonomes et à leurs formes de pensée celles-ci étant le résultat de celles-là, la conséquence toute naturelle de leur façon de sentir ... Pour Marcel l'habitude de penser est si forte chez ses héros qu'elle détermine leurs actes.

In *Les Nouvelles Littéraires,* January 16, 1937, M. Jaloux makes the observation that Marcel's theatre contains a great number of intellectuals. M. Jaloux thinks that this is a mistake, but that it is a mistake that Marcel shares with Stendhal, with Balzac, Flaubert and Zola, as well as with Dostoievsky and Meredith in certain of their works and with Gide in *Les Faux-Monnayeurs.*

Nowhere in Marcel's discussion of his own work does he speak of the class from which his characters are drawn. This fact leads one to believe that Marcel is unconscious that he has selected the majority of his principal characters at least from an intellectual or privileged group.

M. André Bellesort in *Le Plaisir du théâtre* comments on the complexity of the characters and the manner of their communication:

> M. Gabriel Marcel est peut-être celui de nos auteurs dramatiques qui met à la scène le plus d'âmes complexes. Il ne les analyse pas; elles ne s'analysent pas, mais nous entrevoyons, à travers leurs paroles et leurs actes, le va-et-vient de leurs sophismes, de leurs contradictions, des erreurs qu'elles commettent sur elles-mêmes, de leurs aspirations à peine formulées.

M. Luc Estang in *Le Figaro littéraire*, December 17, 1949, compares Marcel's characters with Sartre's characters. M. Estang is quoting M. Jean Hypolite of the Sorbonne:

> "les personnages de M. J.P. Sartre sont entièrement tournés vers l'accomplissement de leur liberté, alors que chez les personnages de M. Gabriel Marcel, du moins chez les principaux, subsiste toujours l'angoisse de saisir leur être."

It is M. Jaloux, in an article in *Les Nouvelles Littéraires*, January 19, 1937, however, who makes a most valid criticism. The article concerns Marcel's habit of bringing into his plays, usually in the final act, the action of Grace. M. Jaloux says that in Marcel's theatre there is nothing lyric on the surface; nothing which recalls the poetry of Maeterlinck or Claudel. Marcel's characters speak everyday language. Even when they say subtle or intellectual things, they do so in an easy or natural way. In this type of drama, M. Jaloux writes: "l'action de la Grâce, qui trouve si naturellement sa place dans un théâtre lyrique et légendaire parait gênée et comme étranglée dans un drame bourgeois." There can be no disagreement with this criticism. It is a *tour de force* which comes as a shock to the spectator, taxes his credulity and threatens the impression of the last act which Marcel has stated is of prime importance in every play. Thus the device is not only a mistake artistically but weakens the entire impact of the dramatist's thought.

The following special characteristics are important and have not so far been mentioned here by Marcel, or his critics.

Male characters often suffer from insufficient power to act and are consequently unable to find satisfaction in their goals; in contrast with the women, always strong, whose very strength often defeats their opportunity for happiness.

Problems, as in most cases in life, are never really solved. Marcel either relegates them to another world or they continue after the curtain descends. Marcel's preoccupation with another world stems from his belief that this universe embodies only part of reality. Thus we have in many plays divine intervention, bringing hope and the suggestion of a final solution.

Sinners are portrayed according to a pattern somewhat

different from that set by other writers. Marcel's sinners are neither so conscious as those of Racine, nor so unconscious as those of Mauriac and Julien Green. They are never completely black nor completely pitiable. Gabriel Marcel has brought to his theatre his own anxiety. He is the embodiment of the anxious man. He is the anxious little boy whose childhood is dominated by the sudden death of his mother. He is the unhappy schoolboy whose every activity, whose failures and successes, assume exaggerated importance to his parents. He is the anxious child, filled with resentments caused by an inflexible system of education. He is the philosopher who shared the "angoisse" of Existentialists. He shared their sincere attempt to deal candidly with the apparent absurdity of life and their doctrine of the liberty of the human spirit and even of man's right to suicide. Along with other French intellectuals, after the terrible experiences of war and occupation, he sought a new and honest philosophy.

But Gabriel Marcel's anxiety could not be assuaged by atheistic Existentialism. He could not conceive of a world without hope and, from the depths of his despair, hope was born. "La structure du monde où nous vivons permet et en quelque façon peut sembler conseiller un désespoir absolu. Mais ce n'est que dans un monde semblable qu'une espérance invisible peut surgir."[5]

Hope implies faith and it is at this point that the student of Marcel's plays may well find himself in disagreement with the author. Marcel's doctrines of religious salvation, and of grace through the Roman Catholic Church may be difficult for many to accept. For him the ultimate solution will not be found except in another world. It is only when this other world is approached either through disillusionment, desperation, illness or death, that man comes close to God and final happiness becomes possible. For many, the plays in which theology and metaphysics have a large role are weakened because of this fact. And even Marcel himself has said that the plays that seem to him to be the most spiritual are absolutely devoid of all "philosophical premeditation ".

It must be said however that this drama is not addressed solely to Catholics or to Christians as are the plays of Henri

Ghéon. Marcel grants an equal degree of efficacy to the other great revelations. Nor does he, though he is so vitally concerned with the problem of grace, find it necessary to depict vice in its most loathesome aspects as does Mauriac in order to demonstrate the miracle of conversion.

The early plays concerned with the problems of faith and grace, just escape didacticism by the presence of flesh and blood protagonists; the middle period is almost entirely devoid of theology or metaphysics; the post-war group speaks for the physically and emotionally displaced, and finally his latest plays, have as their themes social problems of our time. But above and beyond the themes, the psychological penetration, there is the esthetic creation, the mystery and the spirituallity "où le dramaturge nous transporte vraiment dans un monde différente ..." This world is often despairing, reflecting the anguish of our time. Sometimes it seems to reject happiness and insists on the tragedy of the human condition; the essence of poetry is there though Marcel's characters remain in the realm of the real. Through the elevation of his thought and language, he creates a sense of mystery and a kind of illumination, that element that Marcel calls a "résonance éternelle" without which the theatre is sterile.

It is fair to say that the plays of Gabriel Marcel make their appeal primarily on the intellectual level. It is the appeal of a fugue or a sonata. Marcel's plays, subtle yet profound, relentlessly portray the character of man and create acutely moving situations, always expressed in elevated language. This theatre might be rejected by some, but it cannot be ignored. One may sense the affinity with Becque, with Curel, Ibsen, Dostoievsky or Lenormand, but Marcel's theatre is distinctly his own, presented with originality, expressing his personality.

NOTES

[1] P. 35.
[2] P. 13.
[3] Vol. 2, pp. 439-40.
[4] January 9, 1937.
[5] Positions et approches concrètes du Mystère Ontologique, publié avec *Le Monde cassé*, pp. 279-80.

Part Two

CHAPTER III

The Plays

1—Ideological conflicts

La Grâce
Le Palais de sable
L'Iconoclaste
L'Horizon

A study of the plays of Gabriel Marcel makes it clear that the author has correctly stated the dominant characteristic of his drama: man's loneliness in the universe.

In presenting the following twenty plays which represent Marcel's published dramatic work, we shall attempt to show that in each play, man is alone because of his inability to understand his own motivations, and consequently his behavior toward others. The result is bewilderment and tragedy.

In the earliest plays Marcel's characters are not convincing as human beings; but the ideas they express are always concerned with man's loneliness. *La Grâce* and *Le Palais de sable* are Marcel's platform for the discussion of ideas of Faith, Grace and Hope. In *L'Iconoclaste* his concern is with the same problems, only here his recent experiments in the field of spiritualism influence the subject matter. *L'Horizon* is heavily weighted with metapsychical ideas, and is also influenced by his metapsychical investigations. These are plays of ideas, and they are relatively abstract. Marcel, always a critic of drama which is merely the illustration of an idea, desired from the beginning of his writing to express emotion born of intense intellectual experience: "faire vivre dramatiquement les pensées".[1]

37

It would be a mistake to see in these early plays only an intellectual debate. Though the characters do not attain the lifelike quality that is characteristic of the plays which follow, they are not automata and always one feels the striving for understanding, whether the situation be conjugal love (*La Grâce* and *L'Horizon*), parental love (*Le Palais de sable*) or friendship (*L'Iconoclaste*).

It is important to recognize the fact that from the earliest plays the theme of solitude emerges; that keynote of the entire theatre of Marcel, man's loneliness in the universe.

The first play, *La Grâce*, written in 1911, was published in 1914, together with *Le Palais de sable*, under the title, *Le Seuil invisible.* In the Introduction, Marcel says: "... ces pages et les deux drames qui suivent, s'adressent à ceux qui en face des grandes abîmes de la vie intérieure ont éprouvé le frisson de l'infini, à ceux pour qui les idées ne se posent pas seulement comme des lueurs abstraites aux cimes les plus dépouillées de la réflexion, mais pénètrent jusqu'à la moëlle de la vie pour lui infuser le pathétique éternel, hors duquel il n'y a de place que pour les contingences de l'anecdote." It should be remembered that these plays were published fifteen years before Gabriel Marcel's conversion to Catholicism; therefore this preoccupation with religion in a supposed agnostic is all the more remarkable.

The two main protagonists in *La Grâce* are Françoise, an intelligent, healthy, young woman with modern ideas, and her husband Gérard Launey. The action of the play begins before their marriage. Françoise is an unbeliever. She has been working in a psychopathological laboratory with a certain Dr. du Ryer who is in love with her. But Françoise loves Gérard passionately, and when he tells her that their marriage must not take place because he has discovered that he had tuberculosis, she insists that they do not tell anyone of his illness, but marry at once: "Il pourrait disparaître sans que j'aie été à lui".[2] They marry and go to live in Switzerland. The marriage is unhappy from the start because of the basic conflict in their natures. Françoise says: "Celle qu'il aime en moi est une étrangère chaste et craintive que je ne connais pas; j'ai frémi le jour où pour la première fois j'ai compris quelle image étrange il se faisait de moi et aimait à ma place. Et puis poussée par je ne sais quelle puissance irrésistible, je me suis appliquée de toutes les forces de mon être à ressembler à cette image infidèle. La comprends-tu maintenant ma douleur? Comprends-tu ce que c'est pour moi que d'étre obligée de mentir à moi-même et de mentir à celui que j'aime mieux que moi-même, alors que la sincérité est le seul devoir que j'aie jamais compris, le seul que j'aurais voulu pratiquer".[3] Gérard who is "croyant" and whose religious fervor increases with the decline of his health, now makes a fetish of purity:

Françoise.   Comme si je ne savais pas que ta sainteté n'est que l'oeuvre de ta maladie ... Quand tu n'as plus eu la force d'aimer comme les hommes, tu t'es mis à aimer comme les saints ...[4]

With the progress of the illness, faith and mysticism absorb Gérard completely, and husband and wife grow farther and farther apart. Finally, in despair, Françoise becomes the mistress of du Ryer. During a brief period of remission in his illness, the attitude of Gérard changes, and, sensing his wife's misery, he tries to become her lover. She then confesses her unfaithfulness and Gérad, convinced that his desire was only a temptation, cries "... mon Dieu, nous ne sommes pas, et vous êtes. Vous m'avez tenté puis vous m'avez sauvé ... une fois de plus je sens monter en moi la sève des âmes renouvelées". "... les voies de la Grâce." Olivier, the young brother of Françoise who is preparing to enter the Church, is with the couple when Gérard is dying.

The reader is left here to struggle with the problem as in the case of many of Marcel's plays. Does Marcel support Gérard who sought to deny the demands of the flesh? Or are his sympathies with Fançoise, whom he seems to have drawn more sympathetically? Françoise acknowledges that there is more to life than the body when she says to du Ryer: "Avez-vous réfléchi, qu'un individu, malgré tout, est autre chose que l'ensemble des phénomènes que vous décrivez, que vous prétendez analyser?"

The tragedy of Françoise and Gérard, attracted to each other, loving one another, but not with the same kind of love, and never at any time finding themselves on the same plane of existence, is a common one in Marcel's theatre. Whether in 1911 when Marcel, the young agnostic, wrote this play he was chiefly concerned with the frustrations of life as embodied in these two, remains a question. When I asked him whether he considered Gérard worthy of grace he answered: "Grace is given regardless of worthiness, and Gérard's illness brought him insight. There is a connection between illness and Grace. Illness is a means used by Providence."

A break in the clouds at the end of a play, in this particular one, the hope symbolized by Olivier, is used by Marcel throughout his theatre; and in his second play, *Le Palais de sable,* we shall see it again.

La Grâce contains the main characteristics of Marcel's drama. In it he has used his chief themes—illness and death, with the approach of death exerting influence on one of the main characters. He has also used loneliness and lack of communication as a prime motif. But the ideas of Faith and Grace play the most significant roles and at a time when Marcel himself does not know whether he is a Catholic or even a Christian. At this moment Marcel's spirit is torn between opposite poles; he tries to externalize his problem by means of the dialogue between the unbeliever, Françoise, who represents the scientific point of view, and Gérard to whom illness and approaching death have brought keener insight.

Gérard is typical of the Marcel man. His illness is not merely physical; he is afraid of life and love and attracted to the idea of death. We shall meet him again as Claude in *Un Homme de Dieu,* and as André in *La Chapelle ardente* and in many other plays. Françoise is also typical; strong and resolute, she knows what she wants and has the courage to seek it. She chose a career in science though her choice was contrary to the wishes of her family. She married the man she loved in spite of the obstacle of his illness. Because of her love for him she was blinded to his frailties of character; disillusionment and tragedy resulted. Françoise's is the dominant voice in this dialogue. It is the voice which rejects faith as a solution of the problem; though in the end hope is not withheld.

Moirans, the hero in *Le Palais de sable* is a Catholic Deputy. In spite of his successful career, he is a very lonely, unhappy man. His wife plays no part in his life, in fact she is insignificant and disregarded by everyone. The only person whom Moirans really loves is his younger daughter, Clarisse; and when Clarisse tells her father that she has decided to enter a convent, he is overcome with grief determined to oppose her plan. Clarisse has announced her intention on the same day that Moirans' older daughter has told him she is going to get a divorce. Despite the fact that he has just made a speech in the Chamber which was a tremendous success, Moirans feels completely frustrated and disgusted with life. Clarisse has told him that she knows his main reason for opposing her sister's divorce is not a religious one and that he is concerned with the social repercussions it will have. He admits this is true. In fact, though he is a defender of religion, his own faith is ephemeral. Dogmas for him are only "les images qui symbolisent l'idéal intérieur de la religion". His success in his career accents the fragility of his religious position and he has little respect for his constituents, "les imbéciles" who admire him. Clarisse who knows his real sentiments begs him to resign from his position. He says he will do so only if she gives up the idea of entering a convent. He tells her that she is merely trying to satisfy her desire for security and is not motivated by the longing for a life of prayer. He manages to unsettle her faith and she gives up her plan to become a nun but does not draw closer to her father as he had hoped. She devotes her life to her neglected mother with whom she has nothing in common. Then comes Moirans' real desperation; he realizes that it was Clarisse's disillusionment with him and his life which had led her to wish to reject life. Again we have loneliness and frustration as in *La Grâce*.

In his Journal, written September 1913, about the time of the writing of these plays, we see Marcel struggling with the problem of faith.

Pensez-vous qu'on croit à Dieu et à l'immortalité comme on

croit à l'existence des habitants de Mars? ... Pour les humbles oui, ou les simples, peut-être est-ce cela; peut-être chez les âmes déshéritées et les pauvres intelligences, l'espoir fait-il éclore ces mirages ... Mais sur les sommets ardus nulle vision ne fleurit. La foi véritable surmonte l'illusion de l'objet; elle sait qu'il n'est pas de roc tangible auquel les hautes pensées se heurtent. *Nos pensées sont à elles-mêmes leur seule réalité,* elles se refusent à se suspendre aux terrasses interdites d'un monde.[5]

The following dialogue at the end of the play discusses the above lines and seems to refute them.

Moirans.	Mais il faut bien en revenir là. *Les pensées ne communiquent pas.*
Clarisse.	Il t'est commode de le croire, prends-y garde, et c'est cette illusion qui t'a perdu. Il t'a semblé jadis que tu n'engageais que toi seul, tu as voulu ignorer cet au-delà mystérieux où tombent nos actions. Les idées sont des actions aussi ... et elles travaillent hors de nous: lentement, péniblement, elles se frayent un passage, comme une eau souterraine qui désagrège les roches.
Moirans.	Ainsi, serait-ce possible? La solitude même serait une illusion et *l'on n'aurait même pas le droit de penser sa pensée? J'aurais donné à un autre cette puissance atroce de dépendre de moi.* (il se tait accablé).
Clarisse.	Enfin, Père, tu m'as compris; oui, tu m'as donné cette puissance terrible.
Moirans.	*Pour la première fois je me sens esclave!*[6]

The phrase "Our thoughts are their sole reality" is a far cry from acceptance of religion but the struggle in Marcel's soul continues and can be felt through the intensity of the dialogue. Nevertheless hope is expressed again at the end of the play because Moirans, through his suffering, has attained certain insights.

These two plays, though they are by no means among Marcel's best, have particular importance, for the problem they pose is the conflict between liberty and faith.

Family relationships in the second play are typical. There is no accord between husband and wife, no sympathy

between mother and children, and the father and older
daughter are antagonistic. Moirans' love for his daughter
Clarisse seems something other than parental. I asked Mr.
Marcel whether he had implied the existence of incest in the
father-daughter relationship. He answered "No idea of incest
nor any Freudian interpretation; but the same sort of
passionate and exclusive attachment as exists between
Etienne and his father in *Le Regard neuf*".

In *Le Palais de sable* the idea of a dogmatic faith is still far
away.

With *L'Iconoclaste* we come to one of the most agonizing
periods in Gabriel Marcel's life. It began in 1914 with his
work in the Red Cross conducting investigations of soldiers
who had disappeared. He still suffers from this experience, so
frustrating because so little could ever be accomplished.
Each day he received relatives and friends of the lost men.
They pleaded for his help in throwing some light on the
whereabouts of their relatives. Hundreds of poignant cases
revealed to Marcel the drama of human existence. His deep
sympathies were aroused not only by the searches which
ended in the certain news of the death of a soldier but
equally by those which left the status uncertain. During the
winter of 1916-17, Marcel resorted to experiments in
spiritualism and seances with mediums which definitely
convinced him of the reality of metapsychic phenomena. He
tells us:

> Je ne puis douter que les recherches auxquelles je procédais
> m'aient incité à réfléchir sur les conditions de toute enquête, de
> tout questionnaire, et indirectement à me demander comment il
> est possible de transcender l'ordre où l'esprit ne peut procéder
> que par questions et réponses. Ce serait ici le lieu de rappeler le
> rôle que jouèrent dans le développement de ma pensée les
> expériences métapsychiques auxquelles je me livrai au cours de
> l'hiver 1916-17, et dont je devais faire part à Henri Bergson
> quelques mois plus tard. Elles ont mis pour moi définitivement
> hors de doute la réalité des phénomènes métapsychiques; je
> tiens à le déclarer ici d'autant plus catégoriquement que je n'en
> ai pas fait acception dans mes écrits postérieurs au *Journal
> Métaphysique*.[7]

Marcel's efforts to communicate with the dead are

reflected in *L'Iconoclaste* the first of many of his plays in which the dead influence the living. Indeed it may be said that a dead person has the principal role in the play. Jacques Delorme, who has lost his wife Vivienne some years before, has established communication with the beyond. His despair at her death causes him to contemplate suicide but she manifests herself to him and begs him to marry her friend Madeleine Chazot to provide a mother for their two children. Jacques' most intimate friend is Abel Renaudier. Abel had also been in love with Vivienne before her marriage to Jacques and remained passionately in love with her afterwards. Believing her completely in love with her husband, he accepted the situation and tried to live his own life. He comes home after a long absence, visits Jacques, and finds him apparently happy in his new marriage. Abel is filled with resentment and rancor. He regards Jacques' new life as a betrayal of Vivienne and his own sacrifice as having been made in vain. His impulse to revenge Vivienne and himself takes the form of trying to arouse suspicion in Jacques' mind concerning his dead wife's faithfulness, even casting doubt as to the paternity of Roger, Jacques' son. When he learns from Jacques what the circumstances of his new marriage are, he is filled with remorse. In the effort to restore the faith and love for Vivienne that have enabled Jacques to carry on his life, he resorts unsuccessfully to a deception. Jacques has begun to doubt the reality of his communication with Vivienne. He believes now that he has been the victim of an illusion. All seems lost—loves friendship, faith.

During the period when this play was written there is a decided change in the tone of Marcel's *Journal.* As always his concern is with questions regarding faith, but now he seeks particularly its justification: Troisfontaine writes, commenting on this (L'Existence à l'être):

La question centrale, c'est la justification—si l'on peut dire—de la foi. Alors que tant d'esprits glissaient à cette époque du catholicisme au modernisme, Marcel—et ce n'est pas le moindre intérêt de son odyssée, *remonte la voie* en sens inverse.

In what seems to be a reversion to his own childhood, Marcel has two of the protagonists in *L'Iconoclaste* say:

Jacques.	D'ailleurs je ne comprends pas que tu n'aies pas de scrupules à parler de Dieu aux enfants, toi qui n'as aucune croyance religieuse.
Madeleine.	Comme tu es drôle, Jacques, c'est toi-même qui m'as demandé de le faire.
Jacques.	Je t'ai dit simplement que je ne voulais pas qu'ils fussent élevés comme je l'ai été moi-même, dans l'ignorance de tout ce qui touche à la religion.

Marcel's state of mind at that time, his vacillation between doubt and faith is expressed in the following words of Abel:

Abel.	Oui, je suis certain que je mourrai bientôt. Quelquefois je n'éprouve en face de la mort qu'une sorte d'étrange, de religieuse curiosité. [...] A d'autres moments je me dis que mourir c'est peut-être seulement ne plus rien savoir, devenir une chose, et que nous n'aurons même pas l'affreuse satisfaction de reconnaître que tout est illusion. Mais il m'arrive aussi de prier éperdument, et j'ai alors le sentiment que mes prières font naître en moi une vie nouvelle qui peut-être persistera ... Même quand je ne serai plus là, il me semble que ceux qui m'ont aimé pourront encore quelque chose pour moi et que moi aussi, par une sorte d'échange mystique.

A further illustration of Marcel's vacillation is found in the following dialogue between Abel and Madame Renaudier, his mother:

Mme Renaudier.	Tu es bien un être sans religion.
Abel.	Tu crois? Qu'est-ce donc que la religion ... sinon l'esprit de fidélité? ...
Mme Renaudier.	Tu foules aux pieds les lois divines ... Tu as toujours partagé tes ironies entre l'irreligion de ton père et moi foi catholique.

When we discussed this play Marcel said "*L'Iconoclaste* shows the dualism in my own soul; the need for personal satisfaction through communication. But one must transcend communication, for there is a relation between the living and the dead which transcends physical communication. It is a mystery sensed before it is understood philosophically".

The play leads us to the threshold of the unexplained and the unexplainable; but the thing of prime importance is that the characters are never left absolutely without hope. A faint light burns and though Marcel has plumbed the depths of human suffering, the sense of utter despair is lacking. At the end of the play, Abel says: "Nous avons cheminé dans les ténèbres, mais voici que pour quelques secondes ce passé d'erreurs et de souffrances m'apparaît dans une lumière qui ne peut pas tromper. De toute cette confusion on dirait qu'un ordre se dégage ... Oh! pas une leçon; une harmonie."

It must be noted that the character portrayal in this play lacks the flesh and blood reality of most of the other plays. One must conclude that Marcel was not concerned here with the presentation of his ideas.

At the time he was writing this play Marcel was searching for two things; the possibility of reaching the dead and a firm belief to which to attach himself.

It is curious to note that he did not give up his interest in communication with the dead when he formally accepted the Catholic faith. In an article published in 1938 in *Existentialisme chrétien*,[8] nine years after his conversion and fifteen years after the publication of *L'Iconoclaste*, he wrote:

> On pourrait être tenté de croire que ma conversion au Catholicisme a correspondu pour moi à une répudiation plus ou moins complète des préoccupations qui étaient les miennes dans ce domaine au lendemain de la guerre. Ce serait absolument inexact. Je demeure toujours aussi persuadé que le philosophe est tenu de prendre les faits métapsychiques en considération, et qu'il ne pourra les assimiler qu'à condition de se dégager d'un certain nombre de préjugés spéculatifs. Cette recherche présente d'ailleurs justement cet intérêt de l'obliger à prendre conscience de ces postulats souvent tout implicites.

It is impossible to appraise *L'Iconoclaste* as a play. It lacks life almost completely—and the characters are not typical of Marcel. It is therefore not possible to measure this play with the same yardstick one applies to the others.

The fact that Edmond Jaloux has been able to compare *L'Iconoclaste* to Giraudoux's *Intermezzo* shows that he does not consider the characters of this play as representing living people but as mere pretexts for a certain *Marivaudage*; a "Marivaudage philosophique": "Il y a même dans *L'Icono-claste* un Marivaudage funèbre comme il y en a dans *l'Intermezzo* de M. Jean Giraudoux".[9]

L'Horizon was written in 1928. Writing about the play in 1944, Marcel says:[10] "A la juger superficiellement on pourrait être tenté de penser que toute préoccupation religieuse en est absente; en réalité, ce ne serait pas exact. Et l'importance particulière que je tends encore aujourd'hui à attacher à cet ouvrage tient en partie au fait qu'il illustre d'une façon caractéristique les méthodes d'approche indirecte auxquelles j'ai été amené à recourir à maintes reprises, et cela, si je puis dire, pour mon usage personnel." Marcel adds that the origin of *L'Horizon* was without any doubt the result of experiences he had at l'Institut Métapsychique. When he became acquainted with the extraordinary faculties of a certain Pascal Forthuny:

J'ajoute qu'il me semble avoir pu constater dans certains cas particuliers que le don de voyance de Forthuny s'exerçait parfois sur une personnalité distincte de celle à laquelle il s'adressait. Il existe dans ce domaine des franges sur lesquelles le critique est tenu de concentrer son attention. Je ne relaterai pas ici en detail les faits dont j'ai été témoin; je me bornerai à dire qu'ils n'ont pas seulement mis pour moi définitivement hors de question l'existence de la clairvoyance, mais qu'ils ont encore contribué à me faire reconnaître l'aptitude accordée à quelques sujets exceptionnels de percer en certains points le voile de l'avenir. Au surplus, ma conviction dans cet ordre d'idées était déjà faite en 1917, et je n'ai jamais cessé de penser depuis lors que si l'on s'obstine à contester des faits patents, ce ne peut guère être qu'au nom de postulats dont la philosophie se doit de dénoncer l'arbitraire, et, en fin de compte, de simples préjugés.[11]

This play concerns Germain Lestrade, a doctor, who has chosen to limit his practice to a very few patients. He possesses independent means and is not much interested in working. His wife Thérèse who had been a music teacher before their marriage, finds life with him a rather boring

affair. Germain's closest friend, Bernard Devèze, shares
many of Thérèse's interests, often takes her to concerts and
under different circumstances, could have been in love with
her. Thérèse feels for Bernard a kind of "camaraderie
sentimentale". There is a certain Valentine Merlin, a young
widow, very much in love with Bernard, whom Germain had
been urging Bernard to marry. When the play opens,
Germain is concerned with the problem of what would
become of his two children in the case of his death. He
senses his wife's boredom with their too conventional life
and fears she would be tempted at his death to kick over the
traces and perhaps marry a type like the young composer,
Marc Villars, for whom she has expressed admiration. Is it
not Germain's duty to do something about this while there is
still time? He now begins to think of Bernard as a second
husband for Thérèse. One day Germain and Bernard go to a
seance given by a celebrated medium who predicts that
Germain will be killed in a street accident. Two other of this
man's predictions come true and confirm Germain's belief in
the medium. Germain is sure that his death is imminent. His
preparations for the future become urgent now. But the
prophecy is fulfilled rather by the death of Bernard who is
struck and killed by an automobile on leaving the home of
Germain.

In *L'Horizon* Marcel again uses the death theme. This
time he approaches it indirectly and from an entirely new
angle. In 1917 as we have seen, Marcel had become
interested in clairvoyance and experimented with it. In 1928
he is still firmly convinced of its powers and the fact that
certain people are particularly endowed with clairvoyant
insight. Unlike the use of this theme in *L'Iconoclaste* where
the principal character establishes contact with his dead wife,
in this play the veil of the future is pierced and the
protagonist anticipates his own death.

Marcel says of the plot of this play:

Il s'agissait uniquement pour moi de placer un être en face de la
certitude de sa mort imminente. Pour des raisons faciles à
discerner, il ne pouvait être question de le mettre en présence
d'un pronostic médical. La situation du malade incurable est en

tous points différente de celle que j'avais à poser ici. Je reconnais d'ailleurs qu'en procédant comme j'ai fait, je risquais de me heurter à un certain scepticisme chez des spectateurs peu enclins à admettre l'existence des phénomènes métapsychiques. Mais je ne crus pas devoir tenir compte de cette objection. Je me jugeai en droit de demander au spectateur de m'accorder une telle donnée, au moins à titre de postulat. Mais il faut bien le comprendre, c'est seulement à *partir* de cette donnée que surgit l'ensemble des problèmes autour desquels l'oeuvre se noue.[12]

What are these problems? First, Germain has been guilty of breaking a profound law. It is the law which forbids anticipation. Having broken this law, the frustrations in Germain's life become exaggerated. His wife's indifference towards him changes to scorn bordering on hatred. It appears that he has risked all and gained nothing. But this is not completely true.

Marcel has told us that if the play is judged superficially, one might think that all religious preoccupation is absent. In reality Marcel demonstrated his belief that death itself or the imminence of death sharpens the perceptions, and ennobles the spirit. In this case the transformation is not accomplished through the supposed imminence of Germain's death but by the death of Bernard, his friend. The glimmer of faith and hope is illustrated in the final lines of the play.

Thérèse.	C'est étrange. C'est comme si la réalité de sa mort venait seulement de nous atteindre.
Germain.	Pas seulement de la sienne ... On n'apprend la mort que dans la piété. C'est comme si quelque chose s'était dissipé ... une vapeur affolante ... Thérèse, il était notre ami. Nous l'aimions bien. Nous ne le verrons plus.
Thérèse.	Une chaînon qui manque: que voulait-elle dire?
Germain.	Un instant, j'ai cru comprendre, je ne sais plus ... Je ne méprisais pas Bernard, je l'aimais ... et c'est pour cela que j'ai voulu le rapprocher de toi.
Thérèse.	Tu l'aimais et tu le méprisais; tu m'aimes et tu me détestes. Tout est vrai. Mais comment vivre si l'on ne choisit pas?

Germain.   (Un silence.)
Je partirai avec toi: maintenant qu'il ne s'appartient plus, peut-être nous viendra-t-il en aide ...

In speaking of this play seventeen years later, Marcel says, "L'amour et la douleur, articulés en présence de la mort, semblent nous dispenser un message, une vérité d'illumination, et arracher au moins pour un instant ceux que l'éclair éblouit, à la prison où ils poursuivaient leur tatonnante, leur aveugle prospection."[13] Thus we find Marcel's attitude toward life and death, faith and grace, the same as in 1911 when he wrote *La Grâce* and *Le Palais de sable*. His preoccupation with these problems is still compelling though there is nothing in *L'Horizon* to indicate his impending conversion. Nor do the plays immediately preceding this one make any reference to it.

In connection with this play, Marcel has written the following paragraph illustrating some of the differences between his philosophy and that of Sartre and some others:[14]

Aujourd'hui, en reprenant contact avec cette pièce composée il y a quelque seize ans, il me semble que j'y vois une illustration de cette vie sans la grâce que certains admirateurs, même chrétiens, de J.P. Sartre le louent d'avoir évoquée d'une façon stylisée dans *Huis Clos*. A la vérité, je contesterais formellement que cet ouvrage, dont j'apprécie comme il sied l'âpreté strindbergienne, nous présente un tableau fidèle d'une vie infra-, ou pré-, ou certains diraient même supra-chrétienne. Ce qu'il nous offre, c'est l'aspect outrancier d'un monde où chacun guette au fond du regard de l'autre l'image qui le justifiera à ses propres yeux; on n'a pas signalé, à ma connaissance, l'analogie frappante que présente une telle vision avec celle qui s'étale dans la *Danse devant le miroir*, de François de Curel. Dès lors, c'est la notion même de relation interpersonnelle qui se trouve attaquée et comme dissoute; c'est le nous qui est sinon nié, tout au moins réduit à ses expressions les plus indigentes. Et surtout, ce qui est radicalement nié, c'est le dynamisme intérieur en vertu duquel une relation humaine reste, malgré tout, susceptible de s'intimiser et de se dépasser. Dira-t-on que ce dynamisme, c'est precisément la Grâce? Mais on serait alors amené à avouer ce que pour ma part j'accorderais très volontiers, mais ce qui me paraît peu compatible avec la position métaphysique d'un

Sartre, qu'en dernière analyse l'humain lui-même, pour s'affirmer ou se maintenir en tant qu'humain, pour ne pas déchoir irrémédiablement, suppose un principe qui le transcende et qui ne se laisse pas réduire aux données de la raison naturelle.

The four preceding plays, though they lack the dramatic quality of later plays are more than mere expressions of ideas. The dominant characteristics of Marcel's theatre are already indicated: man's loneliness and his struggle to understand himself and his fellowman; his eagerness to find Faith and Grace, and his need to hope. The extraordinary situations in *L'Iconoclaste* and *L'Horizon* which were the result of Marcel's experiments in the field of spiritualism, add to the effect of abstractness in these two plays.

But the plays are neither thesis plays nor philosophical dialogue. The action is not directed by any preconceived doctrine: it is derived from man and not theories. Marcel's protagonists portray intensely a human situation which usually can be analyzed only later on the plane of reflection. His complex characters, though often expressing the convictions of the author, are not the mouthpieces for systems of thought; they express the ideas of thinking human beings in a world of action. Characters such as Gérard in *La Grâce* and Clarisse in *Le Palais de sable* are people for whom the world of ideas is a very real world. Gérard says "Nous sommes des idées"; and Clarisse "Nos idées sont des actions." For them the world of ideas and the world of reality are one.

2—Conflicts reflecting World War I

La Chapelle ardente
Le Mort de demain
Le Regard neuf
Le Monde cassé

In the next group of plays, family conflicts and hostilities constitute the subject matter. In each of these plays World War I is reponsible for the particular situations and dislocations; but in all of them the central problem is the difficulty of understanding human actions and of judging these actions with charity. Most of the characters are avid for tolerance, forbearance and love; but vanity, one of the defenses raised against human frailty, often stands in the way. Few religious or metaphysical problems are discussed here, but the soul remains "in exile"; man is alone.

* * *

La Chapelle ardente opens with Theme I—the influence of the dead upon the living. The dead person is Raymond Fortier, killed in World War I.

Aline, his mother, is devoting her entire life to preserving the memory of her dead son. She considers any activity of the rest of her family which does not directly concern Raymond as a breech of faith with the dead boy. Raymond had been engaged to marry Mireille Pradol, a fine young woman, who is now a visitor in Aline's country home. Aline's attitude has made a strong impression on Mireille, to the extent that she has refused to marry Robert Chanteuil, an attractive young man who loves her and to whom she is attracted. Aline pretends that she wishes Mireille to rebuild her life, but her disapproval of Chanteuil is apparent to the girl. Aline would like Mireille to marry her nephew André, whom she does not love, who is ill with a serious cardiac disease. The idea of this marriage is acceptable to Aline, whose resentment is directed against the strong and well. At first Mireille resists.

Mireille,	(avec violence). Alors, tu t'imagines que je songe à commettre ce suicide? Je maintiens le mot: suicide. Et ça ne te fait pas horreur? Tu admets de sang-froid que je puisse épouser ce moribond ... pour qui je n'ai qu'un peu de pitié et peut-être aussi du mépris? ... Ah! si mes parents étaient encore de ce monde, ils ne le permettraient pas, ils me défendraient contre moi-même.[15]

But Aline is too strong for the younger woman and the marriage takes place. Meanwhile Aline's husband Octave has left her, chiefly because of her role in forcing the marriage which he considers a crime.

A year later we find Mireille and her husband André established in their Paris apartment. André's health has improved but Mireille is in a depressed state following a recent miscarriage. A telegram arrives from Aline announcing her intention to pay the young couple a visit, her first since their marriage. André suggests that they invite her to stay with them but Mireille objects to this. André asks if they do not owe a debt to Aline. Mireille answers "Nous n'avons pas de devoirs envers elle. Il y a un fait, c'est que la vie n'est supportable que si elle est loin".[16]

Aline arrives and loses no time in telling the young couple that Chanteuil, the man who was in love with Mireille, has been killed in an automobile accident and adds that "elle, la personne qui était avec lui a été grièvement blessée". This final bit of information is the last straw for Mireille.

Aline.	Mais tu pleures! tu pleures! tu te mens à toi-même. (Mouvement de Mireille.) Mon petit! Alors, c'est vrai! C'est ma faute! et ce malheureux Chanteuil, peut-être …
Mirielle,	(avec une sorte de rage). Mais qu'est-ce que tu cherches à me faire dire? Tes remords font autant de mal que ta tyrannie! Ah! je te déteste! … était-ce pour mieux détruire que tu es rentrée dans cette chambre? Est-ce que tu as eu peur qu'il ne restât ici un tout petit peu de vie? Non, non, pas ces yeux de victime … Ah! tu es effrayante; quand tu nous as brisé le coeur, tu viens encore nous forcer à te demander pardon!

Aline now leaves to go to the Lutétia Hotel after declining André's invitation to remain in the apartment, and André asks Mireille:

	Tu crois vraiment qu'elle est méchante?
Mireille.	Non. C'est une pauvre femme. (Un silence.)
André.	Elle a dit adieu.
Mireille,	(avec angoisse). Tu es sûr qu'elle a dit adieu?

	Elle ne peut pourtant pas avoir l'idée de ... n'est-ce pas? ce n'est pas possible?
André.	Mais ...
Mireille.	C'est qu'elle a tant souffert ... En somme, qu'est-ce qui la retiendrait? ... Elle n'est pas croyante ... Et alors, si elle, André, si elle se tuait ... (Avec égarement.) La vie ne serait plus possible. Il faut à tout prix ... (Un silence. Mireille va à la table-bureau et cherche quelque chose.)
André.	Que cherches-tu?
Mireille,	(avec une sorte de résignation accablée).- —Le numéro de Lutétia.[17]

Marcel believes *La Chapelle ardente* occupies a particular place among his dramatic works. He says *"La Chapelle ardente* m'est toujours apparue comme une des plus significatives parmi mes oeuvres dramatiques—en partie d'ailleurs parce que les références philosophiques y sont *moins* visibles peut-être que partout ailleurs. C'est là, me semble-t-il, du *théâtre pur* en admettant que ce mot ait un sens".[18]

It is in this reference, apart from any religious or philosophical implication, that the play should be appraised. Aline Fortier is one of the great characterizations of Marcel's theatre. Her only spiritual descendant appears in *Le Chemin de Crête* in the character of Ariane who will be discussed later. Aline Fortier's compulsion to destroy was not brought about by the situation—the death of her son, but is an integral characteristic of her personality. She had always exhibited a pathological penchant for unhappiness and death. In an earlier version of the play called *Le Sol détruit* where Marcel has dealt somewhat more kindly with her, she calls happiness "l'apanage des médiocres". In the final version André quotes Raymond, the dead boy, as having once said "C'est curieux, maman est quelqu'un qui aime les malheureux—moi, ils me font peur." But mama not only loved the unfortunate, she found it necessary to create the misfortune; and to be very certain that she had done an effective job. During the first hour of her visit to Mireille she said,[19]

	Quand j'ai sonné tout à l'heure, tu ne te doutes pas de l'angoisse ...
Mireille.	Si, si, je sais ...
Aline.	J'ai quelquefois si peur que tu ne sois pas heureuse ...
Mireille,	(avec sécheresse). André est très bon ... il m'aime tendrement. J'ai la vie que j'ai choisie ... (Avec une violence soudaine.) que moi j'ai choisie.
Aline,	(malgré elle). Tu en es tout à fait certaine?
Mireielle.	Je ne te permets pas d'en douter.
Aline,	(comme si elle avait reçu un coup). Mon Dieu!

Aline also effectively alienates her husband, her daughter and son-in-law who are minor characters in the play. Still another twist was added in *Le Sol détruit*. In a letter written by Raymond to his mother just before his death, he said "C'est comme pour Edmée ... Je découvre que je ne pourrai pas lui écrire, parce qu'Edmée en comparaison de toi, je sens tout de même trop fortement que pour moi c'est la nouveauté, l'inconnu, et en ce moment tout ce qui n'est pas absolu, indubitable, semble se retirer de moi. Je ne sais pas ce que fera Edmée après ma mort, je ne sais même pas ce que je souhaite qu'elle fasse. C'est l'inconnu, tu vois, même en moi. Tandis que toi ..."[20]

Of this earlier version Marcel has written, "Sa valeur dramatique intrinsèque me paraît indéniable. Mais elle jette la pièce par terre par la façon dont elle transforme la relation entre les deux femmes, en éveillant un sentiment d'amère jalousie chez la jeune fille pour la mère de son fiancé. C'était là vraiment une situation impasse; et je vois mal comment la pièce aurait pu continuer".[21]

La Chapelle ardente was produced for the first time on the twenty-fifth of September, 1925, by Le Théâtre des Jeunes Auteurs at the Théâtre du Vieux Colombier and later that same year at the Théâtre de Rochefort. It was revived in 1951 and although it met with some enthusiasm, its affiliation with the "School of Silence" of Vildrac and Jean Jacques Bernard seemed to date it.

The critic, M. Gautier disagrees. He asserts that the play is dated.

> La voilà qui revoit, aujourd'hui, les feux de la rampe, suscitant l'enthousiasme des jeunes comédiens qui l'interprètent comme une chose nouvelle. A nous, ses défauts apparaissent aussi netttement que nous apparaissaient, jadis, ses qualités. Elle date. Elle appartient au théâtre des phrases non terminées. Son dialogue pâtit de trop de points de suspension. A présent, nous aimons moins les mots "souffrance" et "torture", appliqués à des remous d'âme. Nous trouvons ces personnages complaisants pour leurs problèmes.[22]

Lalou, on the other hand also discussing the play at the time of its revival, sees in it the first signs of an evolution. This is the first time Marcel is preoccupied with the effects of war on people.

> Il me semble point qu'Aline aurait prétendu envoûter tout son entourage dans le culte d'un mort si le fils qu'elle pleure n'avait été tué à l'ennemi.
> Si donc nous croyons pouvoir marquer une évolution dans l'oeuvre dramatique de G.M., il conviendra d'en trouver les premiers signes dans cet ourvrage qui date déjà d'un quart de siècle. Sur cette tragédie familiale, conduite avec une inflexible rigueur, pèse déjà l'ombre sinistre de la guerre mondiale.[23]

Le Mort de demain did not follow until 1931. It is a short three act play which Marcel wrote between the sixth and twelfth of December 1919. The action takes place during the war in the autumn of 1916. Noël Framont is fighting at the front. Jeanne, his wife, and their two children are living with Noël's mother, his sister and his brother Antoine, a widower who is now about to remarry. Jeanne is convinced that Noel will be killed in the war and is already thinking of him as dead. When he comes home on an unexpected leave wearing the Croix de Guerre she receives him as a stranger, refuses him her body though she has always passionately loved him. Noël is completely frustrated and bewildered by her conduct and goes to visit Rosine de Murçay, a former mistress. He is finally himself convinced that he will be killed when he goes back to the front and that Antoine his brother will take his place and be father to his children. He leaves home to return to the front with little will to resist what he considers will be his fate.

Though this play does not rank among the more important of Marcel's dramatic works, the situation is indeed a unique one and certain scenes have a poignant quality. For example the following scene between husband and wife:

Noël.	Et alors? (Jeanne va à lui, s'arrête tout près de lui, lui prend les mains, le regarde.) Tu ne dis pas un mot.
Jeanne,	(tout bas.) Je ne peux pas.
Noël.	Tu n'es pas encore remise de cette arrivée trop brusque. J'ai télégraphié de Creil, mais je savais bien que ma dépêche arriverait après moi.
Jeanne.	Ne dis rien. Reste près de moi, comme cela …
Noël.	Mon pauvre trésoir, je ne te trouve pas une mine brillante, sais—tu?
Jeanne.	Je vais très bien, je t'assure.
Noël.	J'ai bien vu à tes lettres que cela n'allait pas. De pauvres lettres de rien.
Jeanne.	Il ne faut pas m'en vouloir.
Noël.	Sans aucun détail. Rien que sur les enfants; les indigestions d'André, les colères de Pierrot. Ça ne suffit pas, tu sais. Sur toi, rien.
Jeanne.	Il n'y a rien à dire.
Noël.	C'est au point que je commençais à me demander si tu ne me cachais pas quelque chose … une maladie …
Jeanne.	Non.
Noël.	Les lettres, là-bas, c'est presque tout …
Jeanne.	Pardon.
Noël.	Ce n'est pas que nous ayons été malheureux tous ces temps-ci.
Jeanne,	(d'une voix altérée.) Tu as failli être tué le 26.
Noël.	Moi?
Jeanne.	Ce n'est pas la peine de mentir. Cottier m'a tout raconté.
Noël.	Quel imbécile! … Je lui donnerai un de ces suifs …
Jeanne.	J'aime mieux savoir. Tu ne me crois pas?

Noël.	Je veux pourvoir dire ce qui me plaît, et rien que ce qui me plaît.
Jeanne.	Comment veux-tu que j'aie confiance, alors?
Noël.	Enfin tu vois, mon grand, je m'en suis tiré une fois de plus, et ce sera comme cela encore la prochaine fois. Et en attendant me voici décidé (il baisse la voix.) à fabriquer à André et à Pierrot une gentille petite soeur. Quand je te dis que je suis en forme ... (il lui parle à l'oreille.)
Jeanne,	(avec un mouvement de recul.) Non, non ... je ne veux pas, je ne peux plus ... (Elle éclate en sanglots.)²⁴

While Jeanne's reaction to Noël is quite the opposite of
what one would expect from a faithful and loving wife, it is
not impossible to imagine. It is an ordinary and human
quality to fear the worst; and it needed only a step from
beliving that her husband would be killed for Jeanne to
imagine Noël as no longer a part of this world. Also, it is
possible, that if Noël's return had not been unexpected she
might have become accustomed to the idea and behaved in a
normal manner. It is not unusual for people who have loved
each other deeply, to need time, after a separation to resume
their former relationship.

Marcel has said that Jeanne has broken a profound law
which forbids anticipation and in this respect an analogy can
be made between this play and *L'Horizon.*

Une analogie pourrait d'abord être relevée entre *L'Horizon* et
Le Mort de demain. Germain Lestrade, comme Jeanne
Framont, est amené à se rendre coupable d'une infraction
précise à une loi profondément inscrite au coeur même de notre
condition. Cette loi est ce qu'on pourrait appeler le devoir de
non-anticipation; à la base de cette infraction, comment ne pas
discerner une impatience, une intolérance radicale en présence
de l'incertitude à laquelle nous condamne notre existence d'êtres
engagés dans le temps? A cette incertitude à ce ballottement
perpétuel entre l'espoir et le désespoir, Jeanne Framont se
montrait à la longue incapable de résister; elle préférait encore
s'établir dans la conviction que Noël, son mari, serait tué à la
guerre, et cela en dépit, ou plutôt en raison même de l'amour
passionné qu'elle lui portait. Tout se passe, dirais-je, comme si

Jeanne s'installait dans cette certitude pour pouvoir entretenir
avec Noël le rapport défini, univoque, et d'ailleurs unilatéral, qui
lie chacun de nous à "ses morts". Voilà pourquoi elle éloigne
d'elle son mari, pourquoi l'idée d'un contact charnel lui est
devenue insupportable: comment se résoudrait'elle à se donner à
un être qui, demain, n'appartiendra plus à la terre, qui par
conséquent dès à présent a cessé de lui appartenir? car enfin,
cette opposition entre la réalité d'aujourd'hui et celle de demain
est inassimilable pour l'esprit et pour le coeur; on ne peut que le
rejeter comme on lâche un tison incandescent; elle est à la lettre
"intenable".[25]

Noël's reaction to Jeanne's state of mind is a very natural
one. Jeanne's attitude is completely incomprehensible to one
with his healthy and very optimistic outlook.

Noël.	Qu'est-ce que cela signifie? Je souhaiterais quelques éclaircissements. Prends qui tu voudras, et tu verras s'il y a un homme, un seul, pour te donner raison. Qu'est-ce qu'il y a à comprendre? Que tu ne m'aimes plus, très probablement parce que tu en aimes un autre. Evidemment, telle que je te connais, ces mois de séparation ont dû te paraître longs comme à moi-même. Par conséquent …
Jeanne	Je te défends de répéter cette ignominie … Alors voilà où nous en sommes: voilà l'image que tu te fais de moi; voilà les pensées qui ont mûri en toi à l'ombre de la mort.
Noël.	Qu'est-ce que la mort a à faire là dedans? (un silence. D'un autre ton.) Il y a quelque chose d'odieux dans ta conduite envers moi, Jeanne, il me semble que tu dois le comprendre. Une femme ne reproche pas à un homme de la désirer: tu feins de voir dans ce désir je ne sais quel instinct bestial.[26]

This play, with the death theme as its chief motive,
expresses also the idea of Theme I—loneliness in a world
where it is impossible to understand the heart of another.
Noël and Jeanne, apparently products of the same type of
background, and having had no emotional difficulties in the

past, confronted with an extraordinary situation such as war, suddenly become incomprehensible to each other.

Marcel shows us in the play that the crisis between Jeanne and Noël is more of a threat to Noël's life than the dangers of war itself. "Il est entré ici vivant, il en sortira ... mort." The living person today is sacrified for the dead of tomorrow.

The development of the ideas of Faith and Grace is a negative one and hope seems absent. But the significant thing is that twelve years after the end of World War I and eight years before World War II, Marcel is considering the effects of war on human character. A few years later he was to devote the greater part of his writing to this subject. Indeed in *Rome n'est plus dans Rome,* which he wrote in 1951, he expresses the same idea in almost the same words that he used in *Le Mort de demain,* namely anxiety about the reactions of people living under the stress of war. In the earlier play Jeanne says: "... On ne sait jamais quelle loque le malheur fera de vous. Il faut agir pendant qu'on peut encore ..."[27] In "Rome" he has one of the characters say, "Tu comprends, je ne sais pas du tout ce que l'événement fera de moi, peut-être une loque. Je ne présume aucunement de mes forces. Mais je crois en Dieu, je compte qu'il ne m'abandonnera pas, qu'il m'épargnera la suprême déchéance, et qu'ou bien il me reprendra ou bien il me donnera la force de supporter la torture".[28]

One final comment on this play which is apparently so stark and hopeless, should be made—Marcel's reference to immortality: "... Aimer un être, c'est lui dire: Toi, tu ne mourras pas".[29] If Jeanne's love for Noël's is sufficiently great, he will remain alive for her and perhaps for her children. But this would certainly be little compensation for the very earthy Noël. The play remains one of the most tragic of all the plays of this period.

In *Le Regard neuf* the war is responsible not only for Etienne Jourdain's absence from home but also for the beginning of his maturity. He realizes for the first time the abyss which separates his parents. With the cruelty of youth Etienne disregards his mother and thinks only of the happiness which would come to his father, married to a woman his equal. But Marcel condemns "le regard neuf" of youth and pleads for tolerance in the face of the mediocrity of a sordid domesticity. Elise, the mother is materialistic and vulgar but she is also a human being who suffers; and Maurice, by his disdain has added to their common misery.

Published in 1931 this play had been produced nine years earlier for the first time at the Nouvel Ambigu (spectacle des écoliers). The action takes place in Paris in the sring of 1919. Etienne Jourdain has just been demobilized and has returned to the home of his parents, Elise and Maurice. This couple is living a life of misery. Elise is a wealthy, avaricious woman who shares none of her husband's intellectual interests. Maurice is cultivated and fine, though he had undoubtedly married Elise because she was rich and because he dreaded a life of poverty to which his career as a civil servant condemned him. Both adore their only child but he, Etienne, upon his return sees his parents in a new perspective. He has matured because of his war experience and now he can see the great gulf which separates his mother and father. Father and son grow closer now and the mother, sensing the boy's rejection of her, and her husband's ever more complete estrangement, grows morbidly jealous and impossible to live with.

Elise.	Je ne peux pas supporter que tu sois comme ça avec lui. L'autre jour ... quand nous sommes sortis tous les trois ... vous, naturellement, vous ne vous occupiez pas de moi. Vous causiez. En traversant, tu ne te retournais même pas.
Maurice.	Non, je t'en prie, c'est comique.
Elise.	Personne ne trouverait ça ridicule. Les autos m'affolent, tu le sais bien. Hier encore, avenue de l'Opéra, j'ai demandé à une monsieur de m'aider à traverser. Vous causiez, vous causiez toujours. Ah! vous en aviez à vous raconter tous les deux! De temps en temps je courais pour vous rattraper; je courais, Maurice, à mon âge! Je tâchais de me mêler à votre conversation; je parlais de quelque choise que je venais de voir. Toi, tu ne répondais seulement pas; le petit disait:

"Oui, maman." ou bien: "Non, je n'ai pas
remarqué." et il recommençait à te parler. Et
de nouveau je restais en arrière … Si c'est ça
que tu appelles sortir ensemble! A un
moment tu lui as mis la main sur l'épaule et
vous avez continué tout à fait comme si vous
étiez seuls. Moi je trottais par derrière.[30]

Our sympathy is aroused for this aging, unattractive
woman but the situation is further complicated by the
presence of Agathe Clément, a relative of Elise who has
come to Paris as a refugee and is making her home with the
Jourdains. Agathe is a widow, a woman of taste and
intelligence and she and Maurice have much in common.
When Etienne sees that they are attracted to each other, he
urges his father to rebuild his life with her.

Etienne.	Papa, il ne faut plus me regarder comme tout à l'heure. Ces regards-là font trop mal. C'est déjà bien assez troublant; songe: se retrouver chez soi, en apparence rien n'a changé, et pourtant on n'est plus le même; on revoit tout avec des yeux neufs.
Maurice,	(avec émotion.) Mon petit, c'est vraiment à ce point?
Etienne.	Naturellement, je me demande à présent comment certaines choses ne m'ont pas sauté aux yeux plus tôt. Je suis peut-être resté enfant plus longtemps que d'autres, ou bien … Non, tout de même, cela ne devait pas être tout à fait pareil.
Maurice.	Et cependant, je crois qu'au fond nous n'avons changé ni ta mère, ni moi.
	…………………………………………
Maurice.	… Tu ne te figures donc pas, à présent que tu vois plus clair, ce qu'a été notre vie commune, à ta mère et à moi? …
Etienne,	(avec égarement.) Je ne peux plus … puisqu'on me force à choisir … Oh! et puis le choix était tout fait … ce n'est plus la peine de chercher à tout concilier, à mettre de la colle sur un meuble qui se disloque … je ne peux plus … elle t'accuse maintenant

	devant moi, elle ramasse toutes les injures, toutes les calomnies ... Papa, je te le répète, il n'y a rien entre cette femme et toi, il n'y a rien entre moi et elle.
Maurice.	Mon petit ...
Etienne.	Je ne lui dois rien ... (Brusquement.) Papa, Agathe veut partir; elle veut retourner à Saint-Quentin.
Maurice.	Comment?
Etienne.	Et sais-tu pourquoi? ... parce qu'elle t'aime.[31]

But nothing comes of this attraction between Maurice and Agathe. Maurice is afraid. He has become accustomed to the sordidness of his married life; to change now is impossible for him to contemplate. He also cannot face the loss of material comfort, and divorcing his wife would entail this sacrifice.

Etienne,	(éclatant.) Ainsi, tu es décidé? Tu l'abandonnes? ... Elle n'aurait pas de quoi satisfaire ton goût ... pour le confort. C'est la seule raison, il est inutile d'en chercher d'autres. S'il n'y avaît pas cette raison inavouable qui te rive à ta femme. tu n'aurais pas cherché tout à l'heure à faire vibrer pour m'émouvoir je ne sais quelles cordes rouillées. Et maintenant c'est tellement clair. Ah! je sais maintenant à quoi m'en tenir sur la valeur de ce désintéressement sentimental qui m'exaltait ... Je sais, on n'est pas tout d'une pièce. Eh bien! je me demande si ce n'est pas cette complication même qui me révolte le plus ... On ne peut rien admirer ... on ne sait plus ... (Avec une profonde douleur.) Tu ne trouves rien à répondre ...[32]

The play, like the great majority of Marcel's plays, is almost devoid of action except in the realm of the psychological. It is important in Marcel's theatre for several reasons. Reading it today almost forty years after it was written, it seems contemporary, and there is no possibility of its aging because the characters are so truthfully drawn.

There is no better example in today's theatre of character analysis, frank to the point of cruelty, than we find in *Le Regard neuf*. The immaturity of Etienne is expressed in his inability to comprehend that his father is tied to his mother through the habit of years, however unhappy the relationship has been. Marcel shows us that "le regard neuf" of Etienne is immature. Maurice, once having realized his guilt, can transform his marriage into a relationship of greater dignity:

Maurice. Je devrais dire sous l'action de sa présence ici, ses défauts me sont apparus avec une évidence croissante. Maintenant n'ai-je moi-même aucun reproche à me faire? Tu sais bien qu'il m'arrive d'être blessant, d'être cruel. Il n'y a pas à se le dissimuler: j'ai pu dans une certaine mesure, par mes violences inopportunes et même autrefois déjà par mon dédain, contribuer à aggraver certains dissentiments ... (A mi-voix.) Qui sait ... Peut-être même à l'avilir! ...[33]

Poor Elise may not have the capacity for change but she can be less unhappy. We can leave this family feeling more optimistic about their future than with most of Marcel's families we have met up to this time.

There is no discussion of philosophy or metaphysics in this play, and only one reference to religion. The following dialogue between Etienne and Maurice could express Marcel's state of mind at this period;

Maurice. Je compte sur toi: tu ne peux pas te douter à quel point. Mon petit, je ne sais pas, mais si par hasard tu t'es fait une foi, ce n'est pas assez de dire que je la respecterai. C'est un mot idiot, respecter. Mon bonheur serait d'arriver à la partager. Il dépendra de toi dans une mesure que tu ne soupçonnes pas que je ne vieillisse pas vilainement, lâchement. Il y a dans ma nature ...

Etienne. Mais, papa, je ne sais pas ce que tu imagines, ce n'est pas du tout une foi. Je ne vais a aucune église, je ne suis même pas sûr de croire en Dieu ... C'est le sentiment que le vérité doit être du côté de ceux qui croient. Par exemple, prier. Moi, je ne peux pas prier. J'ai essayé au front; ainsi une certaine nuit dont je te parlerai une fois et dont le souvenir me fait encore frémir ... Papa, je t'en supplie, puisque c'est fini, puisque je suis là. Mais il me semble maintenant que c'est une chose que je ne sais pas faire et que peut-être un jour elle me sera ... donnée ...[34]

The play remains a plea to the young to show tolerance for the aging. This plea is exemplified in the following beautiful lines of Maurice, addressed to his son, "Le temps qui passe, Etienne, l'âge qui vient, la personnalité qui se durcit: ce sont de terribles réalités que tu ne connais pas encore. Peut-être y a-t-il des âmes qui ne vieillissent pas et qui refont perpétuellement dans le soleil de Dieu. Bénis le ciel, mon petit, d'avoir fait peut-être de toi une de ces âmes privilégiées. Mais pour les âmes mortelles comme la mienne, conserves un peu de charité".[35]

"Nous assistons à un gigantesque déménagement; une dislocation totale de l'homme s'accomplit sous les yeux d'une société prise de panique".[36] This statement, spoken by the principal character in 1933 in *Le Monde cassé*, could have been written of our present atomic age. *Le Monde cassé* is the world of the thirties with its accent on speed and pleasure—automobiles, airplanes, bars, tango and jazz—a world still upset by the war which had been fought and by the presentiment of the one to come.

It is in this climate that Christiane Chesnay is living with her husband Laurent, who loves her but whom she married without love. Sometime before her marriage she had a love affair with a young man who decided to become a Benedictine monk just when they were about to be married. At the opening of the play, Christiane and Laurent have been married for several years and have a son who is in school in Switzerland. Christiane has surrounded herself with a group of gay friends who live on the surface and seek excitement through liaisons and divorces, but who are really unhappy people. Laurent takes no part in their activities, holds himself aloof and is very critical of them. His pride causes him to pretend indifference toward his wife and the people who surround her. Laurent's satisfaction derives from the fact that he takes no part in the activities of Christiane and her friends. She is absolutely free to do what she likes while he remains aloof. But Christiane does not desire this freedom and tells him so.

In her unhappiness, Christiane conceived the idea that Laurent has a need to forgive her. This would bolster his "amour-propre" and give him the confidence in himself that she feels he lacks. She therefore pretends to have an affair with Antonov, a crude, vulgar Russian musician. Then she confesses to Laurent and as she had anticipated, he gets satisfaction from pardoning her. However, she feels still further apart from him.

Christiane. ... L'espèce de tendresse compatissante que tu m'as témoignée alors était comme une caricature horrible de ce que j'avais tant souhaité. Et c'est à partir de ce jour que, pour la première fois, je me suis sentie entièrement seule. Sans recours. Même au fond de moi. En t'avilissant, tu comprends, c'est moimême que j'avais avilie du même coup. Gilbert s'est trouvé là à ce moment pour me dire une fois de plus qu'il m'aimait. Dix fois en d'autres temps, j'avais repoussé cet amour avec des plaisanteries, avec des haussements d'épaules. D'une second à l'autre, il a pris à mes yeux une valeur infinie, il m'est devenu indispensable, je n'ai plus eu la force de lui résister.[37]

At the moment when all seems lost for Laurent and Christiane, a sort of miracle occurs. The sister of the Benedictine monk with whom Christiane had been in love, comes to tell Christiane that her brother is dead:

Geneviève. Votre amour, mon frère l'a porté comme sa croix pendant les derniers mois de sa vie, il l'a offert.

Christiane. C'est impossible ... Pourquoi aurait-il vu

	tout d'un coup quand il avait été aveugle … j'allais dire: de son vivant?
Geneviève.	Nous ne saurons jamais au juste. Mais ce que je peux vous dire, c'est qu'à partir d'une certaine date, oui d'un jour précis, dans les notes qu'il rédigeait chaque matin et qu'il n'a pas eu le temps ou la volonté de détruire, il est sans cesse question de vous … J'ai l'impression que c'est à la suite d'un rêve qu'il a fait …
Christiane, *Geneviève.*	(passionnément.) Je déteste tout cela … Christiane, est-ce que vous ne sentez pas que tout une part de vous-même, la plus précieuse, la seule précieuse …
Christiane, *Geneviève.*	(avec ironie.) Mon âme. Votre âme justement. A-t-elle habité votre vie?
Christiane,	(comme malgré elle.) Non, pas elle. Sa caricature. Une fausse charité qui ne m'a dicté que des mensonges. Un faux amour qui allait peut-être … (Un silence.) C'est comme une brusque lumière que je ne peux pas encore regarder. Geneviève, est-ce que ces choses existent? … On ne comprend rien, on ne connaît personne … Et c'est vous qui me présentez maintenant cette espèce de flamme, cette vérité qui pourrait tuer et dont il faudra vivre? Qui vous envoie, Geneviève? qui, dites-le moi.[38]

In the final scene of the play there is a reconciliation between husband and wife. Christiane tells Laurent "ta faute, c'est ma faute; ta faiblesse, c'est la mienne; mon … péché, si ce mot a un sens, tu en as aussi ta part …"[39] and then the line to which Marcel attaches great importance … "nous ne sommes pas seuls, personne n'est seul, il y a une communion des pécheurs … il y a une communion des saints".[40]

In this play Marcel returns to mysticism and metaphysics. *Le Monde cassé* is the first play which he wrote after his conversion. It is obvious that he was influenced not only by the external forces of the world of the thirties but by the emotional experience of his conversion.

The theme of loneliness is applied to almost every character, resounding in various degrees of sonority; and the death motif at the end of the play brings transfiguration accomplished through grace. But chiefly, the play is distinguished by what, for want of a better term, can be called its "seeking quality". Every character is seeking to grasp something in the confusion of a dislocated world. Christiane's so-called gay companions search for happiness in new thrills; Laurent seeks refuge in his "amour-propre" and Christiane, finding no consolation anywhere on earth, seeks religious faith

Christiane.　　　Le reste est affaire entre moi et moi-même et peut-être Dieu, si Dieu existe, et vous savez, après tout, je ne suis pas si sûre que Dieu n'existe pas. J'ai toujours l'air d'être avec vous tous, comme vous tous qui ne croyez à rien, qui vous moquez de tout, sauf de la mort et de la souffrance, car vous en avez une peur affreuse; oh! je ne dis pas ça particulièrement pour vous, mais en réalité, il y a en moi un être que je ne connais presque pas et qui n'est sûrement pas ... un des vôtre ... un être qui se cherche, et qui se trouve en des secondes bien rares du reste, dans un monde inconnu auquel on dirait que vous n'appartenez pas.[41]

Few will disagree with these sentiments expressed by Christiane but there is a large audience who may find it difficult to follow Marcel in the further development in which he includes intervention and relegates the solution of the problem to another world. This kind of device, a sort of "deux ex machina" which he will use again in future plays, weakens them as drama, to say the least. Furthermore the question must arise, and this without any prejudice or bias: is this not aspiration carried to the point of evasion?

The problem for Marcel is clear; having presented an Existentialist world where there is apparently no hope in material expedients, he leads us into the world of the spirit "votre âme, a-t-elle habité votre vie?" His solution may be acceptable to those who believe in a dogmatic theology but it is not admissible to those who seek a rational approach to the world of the spirit.

But more important for this discussion is whether or not at this point Marcel is himself still seeking. Added to his deeply religious spirit there is his active intelligence which will not find an easy way out. And so the search must continue. I believe the plays which follow will prove this.

In the preface to his play, written in 1933, Gabriel Marcel judges it thus: "*Le Monde cassé* n'est pas une pièce à problème, ce serait bien plutôt un mystère. Le drame amène les deux héros à un point où ils s'apparaissent à eux mêmes comme 'engagés' dans une réalité qui les transcende infiniment et qu'ils ne sauraient avoir la prétention de dominer." Edmond Jaloux commenting on this statement adds: "je m'aperçois que ces explications vont donner aux lecteurs le sentiment que les pièces de Gabriel Marcel sont uniquement philosophiques et, par conséquent obscures. Or, il n'en est rien. Je ne dis pas que, si l'on faisait d'elles un commentaire métaphysique, celui-ci ne passerait, pas souvent, par dessus la tête de l'auditeur. Mais ce qui est exprimé dans le drame est parfaitement explicite et ne contient extérieurement rien qui n'appartienne à l'ordre des choses qu'on a l'habitude de voir sur la scène".[42]

"The order of things which one is in the habit of seeing on the stage", certainly includes some of the tours de force which are characteristic not only of *Le Monde cassé* but of other plays of Gabriel Marcel. If Edmond Jaloux had said instead "things that are ordinarily experienced by the average person", there would be much more room for argument. But since this kind of miracle is not an ordinary experience, its inclusion in many of the plays of Marcel does not add to credibility but rather weakens the validity of the plays.

"Si j'avais une critique à adresser à M. Marcel," continues Edmond Jaloux, "je lui objecterais qu'il agit parfois comme tous les écrivains qui tendent a convertir (au sens religieux du mot) leurs personnages, il semble sous-entendre que le fait d'avoir trouvé—ou d'avoir cru trouver—la foi supprime la plupart des problèmes autérieurs à la conversion ... ce qui, dans un roman parait vraisemblable, tout ce qui est expliqué par l'atmosphere d'un chapitre ... prend sur la scène une apparence forcé et gratuite ... il se peut, au surplus, que cette critique s'applique à notre société et à notre temps plus qu'à Gabriel Marcel lui même; l'action de la grâce, qui trouve si naturellement sa place dans un théâtre lyrique et légendaire celui de M. Paul Claudel, par exemple, parait gênée et comme étranglée dans un drame bourgeois".[43]

This seems to be the most important criticism of Marcel's plays. It is an unreal feature of otherwise completely plausible acts on the part of the characters. It taxes the credulity of the reader and viewer, and disturbs the artistic wholeness of the play. This has nothing to do with whether the reader is a believer or a non-believer. The device simply does not have a place in the bourgeois theatre, in plays whose author wants us to believe his characters are real people in a real world.

The question arises as to why Marcel does this. I believe it to be some kind of compulsion. Mr Marcel sincerely believes in the unseen things which influence our lives; it is possible that he feels that he owes it to mankind to dramatize them. Or it is possible that Marcel feels he owes a debt to the Catholic Church. But it seems that only some kind of compulsion would cause him to tamper with the artistic wholeness of his work.

After the war of 1914 many French dramatists wrote plays concerning the disillusionment of the youth in France.[44] In the majority of these plays the accent is on the difficulty which the returned soldier experienced in his adjustment to his family and to the postwar world. It is interesting to note that in Marcel's four post-war plays presented here, only in one, *Le Regard neuf,* does he deal with a returned soldier, and even here the problem of the boy, Etienne, is secondary to that of his parents. In *La Chapelle ardente* the war hero is dead when the play begins, and the chief character in the play is his psychopathic mother. The real theme of *Le Mort de demain* does not concern the soldier returned on leave but the srange attitude of his wife toward him. Since *Le Monde cassé*, written in 1933, is so removed in time from the end of the war, it could hardly be expected to deal with the problem of a soldier recently returned to civilian life.

Thus, though the actual situations in these plays would not have existed had it not been for the war—a son killed in action, a mobilized husband home on leave, the awakened perceptions of a son after his war service, the broken post-war world—the dominant theme for which the war only furnishes the background is loneliness in the world expressed by a character in *La Chapelle ardente*, "on ne peut rien les uns pour les autres. On est seul".

3—Conflicts reflecting marital and family tensions

> *Le Coeur des autres*
> *Le Quatuor en fa dièse*
> *Un Homme de Dieu*
> *Le Chemin de Crête*
> *Le Fanal*
> *Les Coeurs avides*

In the next group of six plays there are constant conflicts and hostilities. Nothing is really resolved, "rien ne finit jamais pour personne",[46] Marcel continues to paint a world in which people suffer because of what they are and what they do to others, and because they lack sympathy and compassion. There is no easy denouement; man remains alone. The protagonists are earthy creatures, struggling with human problems. In almost every case they do not comprehend their secret motives and pride takes precedence over compassion. The questions of Faith and Grace continue to play a part, but not such a prominent one as in the earliest plays. The light of hope burns though sometimes rather faintly. The loneliness of man is still the dominant characteristic of these plays.

* * *

Le Coeur des autres, written in 1919 and published in the

series *Les Cahiers verts* in 1921, was the first of Marcel's plays to be produced on the stage. It is the story of Rose and Daniel Meyrieux. Their marriage is a happy one, but it is happy at the expense of Rose who has completely subordinated herself to Daniel, her dramatist husband. At the beginning of the play Daniel has just produced a successful play in which he used for his theme an intimate family situation.

Before his marriage Daniel had had an illegitimate son by his mistress. Rose, who has been unable to have a child herself, persuades Daniel to adopt the boy Jean when his mother dies. Rose loves the lad but Daniel dislikes him, finds him lacking in refinement, and is even critical of the boy's hearty appetite. Jean has not been told that Daniel is his real father and when he finds it out he cannot understand his father's attitude towards him.

The misery of the boy reaches a climax when he reads, without permission, his father's unfinished manuscript of a new play.

Daniel.	Alors, tu lis en cachette? Voilà tes moeurs, voila ce qui se cache sous ce masque? (Il le prend par les deux bras et la regarde durement dans les yeux.) Et peut-on savoir dans quel but tu as accompli cet exploit?
Jean,	(sourdement.) Je n'avais personne pour me renseigner sur toi, j'ai pensé qu'en lisant ce que tu écris j'en apprendrais peut-être plus long qu'en posant des questions auxquelles on ne veut pas répondre. J'avais raison. C'était la bonne porte.[47]

The boy is convinced that despite some changes in the character of Gilbert in his father's new play, he *is* Gilbert.

After this occurrence, Daniel decides to transfer Jean to the status of a boarder at school rather than to keep him at home. Rose begs her husband not to do so. A few months later Daniel's new play is produced, *L'Enfant taciturne*. It is a great success, hailed even by critics who have not heretofore been friendly. But Rose has become very unhappy over the appearance of the play and tells Daniel that she has not ceased to suffer since she saw the suffering in the boy's eyes, and that she has continued to resent the fact that Jean was sent away to school. Finally, she demands that he remove the play from the stage. Daniel says that this is impossible, as he has a contract, and besides it is useless; the play has been seen and if there is any harm, it has already been done.

Daniel. Et au fond, veux-tu que je te dise? Il est probable que j'ai eu tort (attendant une contradiction qui ne vient pas). Pour nous deux, j'ai eu tort … Si tu avais connu certaines souffrances, certaines vraies souffrances … Seulement c'est toujours la même chanson, pour apprécier son bonheur …

Rose, (dans un cri.) Il n'y a qu'une souffrance, c'est d'être seule. Avec toi, je suis seule, ou je ne suis pas. Sans toi … je serais peut-être moins seule. Si tu ne retires pas ta pièce, je partirai.[48]

But the play is not taken off the stage and Rose who had intended to leave her husband and make a home for the boy, discovers that the boy no longer needs her. At the school he has made a great friend of a certain Rablé, and they have planned to room together the next year. And Rablé "… est fou de théâtre, il passait son temps à me parler de papa, de sa nouvelle pièce".[49] Rablé pointed out to him that "Molière aussi a mis sa propre histoire à la scène. Moi, je ne savais pas".[50]

Shocked to find that the boy does not need her, and fearing to suffer with him as she has done with Daniel, Rose turns back to her husband and the form of suffering with which she is familiar. But her surrender is not without a certain bitterness. She even says that their life together has given her "une âme débile et gâtée" and the following dialogue ensues:

Daniel. Une âme que j'adore.
Rose. Tu avais peut-être raison, elle doit me venir aussi de toi … Ah! je ne sais plus … Tout est trop difficile! (Elle demeure accablée, Daniel s'est agenouillé devant elle et lui a

Daniel.

Rose,

pris la tête dans les mains) Oui, prends-moi
... je t'appartiens, je ne suis pas quelqu'un
d'autre.

Mon trésor! ...

(avec la plus profonde tristesse.) Comprends-
moi, Daniel, je renonce à moi-même, et je le
sais, et je sais aussi que je ne peux pas faire
autrement. Après dix ans de notre vie on
n'est plus assez fort pour penser à soi.
Quand un être en est là ... va ... tu as
raison. Prends-moi. Et quand tu seras à
court de sujets ...[51]

Gabriel Marcel tells us in this play that the heart of others
is impenetrable. No one is completely understandable to
another no matter how close this person seems to be. When
we discussed this play the dramatist said, "The play is a
terrible indictment of literary men. This using of family
drama for our material is what we have to guard against. I
have to, constantly, myself." He said that he is particularly
fond of Rose and remarked in speaking of Jean, "of course,
she needed the boy much more than he needed her."

There is tension in every relationship in this family: no
understanding between father and son; antagonism of the
wife towards the husband, brought to the surface by Daniel's
cruelty to the child; and lack of Rose's understanding of the
boy who needs more acutely the companionship and
approval of his contemporaries than he needs his mother.

The reason for Daniel's dislike of the boy is suggested in
the play:

Rose.

Daniel.

... Quand cet enfant m'a demandé pourquoi
tu n'avais pas épousé sa mère ... que fallait-
il que je réponde?

... Même s'il en vient à supposer que sa
mère n'était pas épousable, ce qui est
l'exacte vérité ...[52]

But the real cause of Daniel's distaste seem to lie deeper.
Daniel is an egoist or perhaps just an artist "c'est toujours en
moi que je regarde, hélas!"[53] Though he demonstrates
affection for his wife, he is completely engrossed in his

career: "L'oeuvre c'est notre éternité à nous autres, le reste appartient au néant."[54]

The boy Jean seems to anticipate another youth in Marcel's theatre, Marc André in *Rome n'est plus dans Rome*. Jean is a far simpler person of course; but in both characters we find the same ability to recover quickly from an injury to the spirit through a change in environment or by the acquisition of a new friend.

Though in this play there is discussion neither of religion nor of metaphysics, the important line in the play, Rose's cry; "Il n'y a qu'une souffrance, c'est d'être seule" reflects Marcel's persisting absorption in the problem of man's loneliness in the world. It is possible that at this period art may have appeared to him as a surrogate for religious belief as it appears to be later in *Le Quatuor* where he says "la musique dit vraie—la musique seule".[55]

In *Le Coeur des autres* as in the preceding plays, man remains alone in a world where people suffer.

In *Le Quatuor en fa dièse* music furnishes the actual background and motivation for the play. One of the principal characters is a composer. Marcel's passion for music led him to conceive of his plays as a composer conceives a symphony. But for him music is more than a matter of technique, as he tells us in "Regard en arrière", "Il est évident d'autre part que la musique m'offrait un exemple irrécusable du type d'unité supra-rationnelle que le drame avait à mes yeux pour fonction essentielle de poser et de promouvoir. Là est bien entendu le sens profond du 'Quatuor en fa dièse', qui occupe parmi mes oeuvres familiales, de la musique et de la réflexion pure".[56]

When *Le Quatuor en fa dièse* opens, Claire Mazeres, the wife of Stéphan, the composer, is about to divorce him because of his infidelities which she can no longer bear. They shared their grief when they lost their only child; they have loved each other. Stéphan begs Claire not to divorce him:

... je t'en supplie, fais l'effort nécessaire pour oublier tous les mensonges dont la société, le théâtre et le roman nous ont farci l'esprit. Est-ce que vraiment il n'y a rien de changé dans nos rapports profonds? Tu sais que non.[57]

... Claire, tu m'aimes! ... et moi je t'adore.[58]

Claire is too proud to allow the situation to continue and tells Stephan

> ... ma décision est irrévocable, et ne cherches-tu qu'à envenimer encore cette querelle en évoquant tout cela. Tout remonte à la surface ... tout le passé avec un goût de poison.[59] Stéphan, (âprement.)—C'est vrai. On dirait que tu tâches d'empoisonner jusqu'au souvenir. Pourquoi t'acharnes-tu à piétiner ce qui fut? Rougir d'avoir aimé! Être honteuse d'avoir été femme! Ah! l'orgueil, tout cela, l'orgueil et rien d'autre. Tu renies ces heures qui furent si belles et ou nous eûmes tous deux le sentiment que quelque chose de spirituel naissait de nous. Lorsque je t'ai joué pour la première fois le thème de l'andante et que je t'ai vue en larmes ... Oui, c'est fini décidément. Toutes ces choses précieuses se décomposent. Ah! je n'aurais pas cru que cela pût mourir aussi![60]

The divorce takes place. A year later Claire is preparing to leave Paris, which has become intolerable to her, to go to Italy. She has been receiving visits from her mother-in-law and also from Roger, Stephan's brother, but she is desperately unhappy. When Roger learns that Claire is going away he begs her to marry him. Thinking he is doing this out of pity, she refuses him. A few months later however they are married. Their marriage shocks their family and their friends and some of the latter even suspect that an intimacy may have existed between Claire and Roger before Claire's divorce from Stephan. The memories of the past weigh upon the couple. Roger misses Stephan and visits him at his parents' home without Claire's knowledge. Claire is suspicious and irritable and neither is happy. One day the Quatuor is to have its premiere. Claire knows every note of this work since its inception. It was during the time of their divorce that Stephan had completed it. Claire goes to the concert, as does Roger, each hiding the fact from the other.

The day following the concert, Claire, during a visit to her mother-in-law says,

Claire.   Avec cette musique qui bientôt cessa de m'offenser, c'est tout le passé qui revivait: ce passé odieux, banni par la force de ma

pensée, émergea soudain par la musique
d'une séduction douloureuse et irrésistible.
Les mêmes mélodies nous hantaient tous les
deux désormais: seulement, tandis qu'elles
éveillaient en lui en écho fraternal, quel nom
donner à ce qu'elles remuaient en moi? C'est
hier, en écoutant ce quatuor, hier soir, que la
hideuse comédie de ma vie s'est enfin démas-
quée. Je me suis vue enfin telle que l'autre
m'avait vue—jadis—et, je vous le répète, je
me suis condamnée ...
... Rien ne s'abolit. Tout ce qui fut sub-
siste—à jamais. Nous cessions de faire attention, et voilà tout. Mais lorsque nous prêtons
l'oreille de nouveau ... J'en viens à me
demander si je n'ai pas aimé en Roger le
frère de Stéphan.[61]

Roger also is shaken by his attendance at the concert:

Roger.	N'en dis pas plus ... Je ne comprends que trop.
Claire.	Et pourtant j'ai bien cru n'être attirée par toi que parce que tu étais différent de lui. Comme je vous opposais l'un à l'autre!
Roger.	Hélas!
Claire.	Comme j'étais sûre de préférer à ses tendresses capricieuses—ton amitié!
Roger.	Tu n'aimais en moi qu'un reflet.
Claire.	Une image ennoblie.[62]

In discussing this play with Mr. Marcel I asked "do you
say in the play that the creation of music is a kind of
religion?" He answered, "art is beyond religion, beyond
morality beyond any kind of judgment." But one should not
stress the analogy between art and religion too strongly.
Claire is a too moral person until the end. She is a prisoner
of the kind of judgment which demands rigid adherence to
right. Music merely takes her beyond her rigid observance of
these categories. For Roger, " 'la musique dit vrai; la
musique seule'."
During this period Marcel wrote very little in his Journal

concerning religion. The following lines from the play indicate the direction of his thinking:

Stéphan.   "Pourtant ce moi profond, est-ce que ce n'est pas la musique même? Une belle mélodie, n'est-ce pas notre plus haute vérité? ..."[63]

"Ne lui devons-nous pas nos plus belles heures, ce qui fut notre raison de survivre?"[64]

"J'ai souvent pensé que tout ce que l'homme s'est déshabitué de croire, ce pour quoi il n'a plus ni paroles ni respect—eh bien, que tout cela a pris comme sa revanche, vous comprenez, dans la musique. Est-ce qu'elle n'est pas comme l'immortalité de tout ce que nous croyons mort—mais qui ne meurt pas? ..."[65]

"... J'ai senti que tout ce qui vaut dans ma vie, ce que j'ai pu connaître de joie et de souffrance vraie, est enfin là absolument réel pour quiconque sait entendre. Mon histoire—notre histoire—mais hors du temps, purifiée, et telle qu'elle serait pour dieu."[66]

It is interesting to compare these lines to the following paragraph from *La Notion de présence chez Gabriel Marcel* by Roger Troisfontaines, quoting Marcel, "La musique, c'était ma vraie vocation, là surtout je suis créateur, C'est elle qui a donné à ma pensée son cadre le plus authentique. J.-S. Bach a été dans ma vie ce que n'ont été ni Pascal, ni Saint Augustin, ni aucun autre auteur. N'est-ce pas du spirituel authentique qui s'incarne dans les expressions musicales les plus hautes qu'il nous soit donné d'appréhender—chez un Bach—chez le Beethoven des derniers quatuors, chez le Mozart le plus dégagé?"[67]

Besides being of great value to explain Marcel's attitude towards music, *Le Quatuor* is a very good play in which Marcel has known how to "plasticiser pour la scène le tragique de pensée qui est son object principal".[68]

Though *Un Homme de Dieu* was not published until 1925, already in 1921 Marcel's Journal indicates that the idea for the play was established firmly in his mind. The central character in these previous sketches was, as he is the definitive version, a Protestant pastor. The wife was essen-

tially the same character as Edmée in the final form. There
are some minor differences which will be pointed out later.

In this play Marcel asks whether we are really what we
think we are, and what motivates our conduct towards
another person. Its theme is again the loneliness of man in
the world and the struggle to reach the heart of another.

Claude Lemoyne is a Protestant pastor, serving his parish
well and untiringly. Years before, in the early years of her
marriage to Claude, his wife, Edmée had had an affair with
another man, Michel Sandier. Claude knew of this liaison.
Osmonde, the child of Edmée and Sandier, is now twenty
years old and Sandier has come back from his travels,
suffering from a mortal illness, wishing to see his child before
he dies. Sandier has seen Claude and Claude tells Edmée she
must grant him permission to see Osmonde:

Edmée.	Tu as déjà tout arrangé dans ta tête! Mais c'est épouvantable. Mais qui es-tu donc? mais tu n'es pas un homme.
Claude.	C'est un mourant.
Edmée.	Alors, pour toi le passé est aboli, non avenu. Qu'il m'ait serrée dans ses bras, qu'il m'ait pressée contre son coeur ...
Claude.	Tais-toi.
Edmée.	Oh! tu peux tout entendre. Ce n'est pas le sang-froid qui te manque quand il s'agit de moi.
Claude.	Mais c'est monstrueux, Edmée, ce que tu dis là ...
Edmée.	Cette grandeur d'âme à bon marché me fait horreur.
Claude.	A bon marché! Mais quand je t'ai pardonné ...
Edmée.	Si tu ne m'as pas pardonné parce que tu m'aimais, qu'est-ce que tu veux que j'en fasse de ton pardon? (Elle éclate en sanglots.)[69]

The fact is that Edmée has never forgiven Claude's having
pardoned her. She saw in his pardon a kind of professional
virtue and felt the lack of real love and of natural jealousy on
his part. She feels him incapable of taking or loving like a

man and she considers that he was the only one who had benefitted through his *amour-propre* from his act of forgiveness. She has suffered ever since. Osmonde is badly adjusted and unhappy and Sandier, whom Edmée felt really loved her, has wasted himself in a life of dissipation. Furthermore, she would never have deceived her husband if he had loved her as a man should love his wife. All of this she tells Claude.

Now the world of this family begins to break down. Osmonde tells her parents that she is going to live with Megal, a married man whose wife is in an insane asylum; and Claude says to Edmée:

	Ce que j'ai dit tout à l'heure était absolument sincère. Maintenant qu'elle nous quitte, il n'y a pas de raison pour que nous continuions à vivre ensemble. Tu as, paraît-il, de grands devoirs envers quelqu'un d'autre. Tu pourras les remplir en conscience désormais. Quant a moi, il est probable que je quitterai le pastorat.
Edmée,	(avec un brusque effroi.) Ce n'est pas vrai.
Claude.	Le peu de forces que je croyais posséder encore, je sens que je l'ai perdu.
Edmée.	La foi ne peut pas te manquer ainsi tout d'un coup, ce n'est pas possible.
Claude.	Je ne sais pas, la foi véritable ne m'a peut-être jamais été donnée.
Edmée.	La foi véritable … rappelles-toi pourtant, quand nous nous sommes fiancés, la façon dont tu parlais de la vie, le ton dont tu disais certains mots … tu étais sincère.
Claude.	J'étais sincère, j'étais heureux.
Edmée.	Tes yeux brillaient, il me semble quelquefois que c'est à cause de ce regard que je t'ai épousé … Autour de moi personne ne parlait comme toi, et ils avaient tous des figures ternes. Toi, quand tu disais ces mots-là, rien qu'à l'accent avec lequel tu les prononçais … c'était comme un monde que tu m'ouvrais.
Claude.	Et la petite m'avouait il n'y a pas dix

	minutes que ces mêmes phrases trop souvent répétées l'avaient éloignée de la foi …
Edmée.	Tu ne me le disais pas.
Claude.	Est-ce que je t'aimais dans ce temps-là? et toi, m'aimais-tu? nous ne nous le rappelons pas, nous ne l'avons peut-être jamais su. (un silence.) C'est sur la foi d'un regard ou d'une intonation que tu as engagé ta vie. Un regard qui promettait … quoi? cette promesse mystérieuse n'a pas été tenue, et voilà toute l'histoire de notre vie commune … Et lorsque je pense à Dieu, c'est pareil. J'ai crus quelquefois qu'il me parlait, et ce n'était peut-être qu'une exaltation menteuse. Qui suis-je? Quand je cherche à me saisir, je m'échappe à moi-même …
Edmée.	La mort ne t'effraie pas?
Claude.	Non, je ne crois pas … C'est tout de même la seule chance de l'homme. Même si ce n'est pas une porte qui s'ouvre.
Edmée.	Tu es plus brave que moi.
Claude.	Tu as peur d'être jugée?
Edmée.	Oui … je ne sais pas …
Claude.	Et moi au contraire … Etre connu tel qu'on est … ou alors dormir.[70]

This rather long quotation from the final act is used because it demonstrates the stark tragedy of the play—the complete collapse of everything of importance in Claude's life. He has lost his daughter; his relationship with his wife is stripped of all illusion and he is on the point of giving up his vocation as pastor. He believes he has lost any religion he ever possessed and is doubtful that true faith had ever been given him. What he believed to be a relation with God was only a delusion. Claude suggests that Edmée join him in a suicide pact and calls death, even though there is nothing beyond, the only hope of man. Surely this has all the characteristics of Existentialism. it could reasonably be supposed that in this period Marcel, who had been attracted to Protestantism, is dissillusioned by what he calls the religious optimism personified in the emphasis on "good works" in the practice of Protestantism. He has not yet found the answer to his search.

The first sketches for this play were done in 1921, eight years before Marcel's conversion to Catholicism. Much later he was to say through his character Marc André in *Rome n'est plus dans Rome*:

> Vous le savez, maman avait souhaité que je sois protestant, oh! d'un protestantisme aussi libéral que possible. J'ai été à l'école du dimanche, j'ai écouté pendant deux ans les sermons du pasteur Bruissillon. J'ai fini par lui demander l'autorisation de lui poser quelques questions. Au cours de cet entretien j'ai découvert que ce pasteur ne croyait pas à la Rèsurrection du Christ. Je me rappelle les mots dont il s'est servi. Il m'a dit ça très simplement, ca a été un coup de massue. Il fallait entendre le Résurrection en un sens symbolique. Purement symbolique.

Pascal. Mon pauvre enfant.
Marc André. Depuis ce moment-la, j'ai pris les protestants en horreur.[71]

Character delineation in *Un Homme de Dieu* runs rather true to form. Edmée is a typically strong Marcel woman and Claude just escapes being the weak Marcel man—just escapes because he emerges a tragic figure. The spark of human dignity is there in "Etre connu tel qu'on est ..." It is interesting to note that Edmée, in spite of her bitterness, in the end tries to bolster Claude's faith in his religious calling and to preserve her own belief.

It is difficult to find the ray of hope in this play unless it lies in Claude's realization of his failure to understand his motivations. This could result—(barring suicide)—in an increasing power to know himself.

The earlier sketches of the play are not of great importance because the basic idea is the same as in the definitive version. Slight changes in background and in milieu, also in the title, which was to have been *Guérisseur* or later *Guérir*, are to be noted. These titles illustrate Marcel's use of irony. His character is a healer who is unable to heal himself and his family. Likewise in an early sketch Sandier, Edmée's lover is a painter, then a doctor; and Osmonde was a boy.

Un Homme de Dieu is one of the striking plays of Marcel

because of the starkness of its theme and the irony of the situation. Edmée married Claude basically because of his faith; and it is his practice of this faith which separates them.

The critics seem to agree to recognize the strength of *Un Homme de Dieu*, "La force du drame," says Lalou, "tient à ce que G.M. y dépeint, étroitement mêlée, quels troubles naissent de l'ambiguité des sentiments et quels doutes impliquent l'idée d'un choix qui rompe avec tout le passé. Mais pour les trois protagonistes le problème demeure d'ordre moral et strictement intime."[72] And Yves Gandon,

Ou bien l'on n'entend rien au théâtre, ou l'on est obligé de reconnaître que cette pièce en quatre actes est une des plus fortes et des plus substantielles qu'on ait vues depuis longtemps ... Ces quelques réserves faites, on ne peut qu'admirer la justesse et la profondeur de l'analyse, la sûreté de la psychologie, le pathétique intérieur des situations. (Eclairé sur ses faiblesses humaines, le pasteur reprendra sa tâche sans illusion. Edmée restera dans le désert moral auquel son manque d'imagination l'avait condamnée.)[73]

In 1936 Marcel published *Le Chemin de Crête*. Ariane Leprieur, the principal character is living apart from her husband Jérôme. Early in their married life, because of an attack of tuberculosis, she was forced to live in the mountains, and now, though she has been pronounced completely cured, she refuses to come back home and resume a normal life. Meanwhile, Jérôme, a journalist, is having an affair with Violette Mazargues, a gifted young violinist with a past. Violette has an illegitimate child whose father Serge Franchard loved Violette and wished to marry her, but she had refused to marry him. Now, Violette is much in love with Jérôme. She does not know his wife Ariane, but she feels a great sense of guilt because of her love for Jérôme.

Violette.	Mon pauvre Jérôme, il y aurait de la bassesse à esperer trouver en elle de quoi justifier notre conduite; elle n'est pas justifiable. Ayons du moins le courage de la reconnaître.
Jérôme.	Je ne pourrai jamais m'y résigner. Toi ... toi

	surtout … Il faut que je puisse me dire tout le temps: c'est sa faute, sa faute à elle.
Violette,	(tristement.) Tu sais bien que ce n'est pas vrai.
Jérôme.	Songes donc, en trois ans elle a passé six semaines à Paris.
Violette.	Rien ne t'empêchait de rester à Logny avec elle.
Jérôme.	Dans ces montagnes que je déteste, qui m'étouffent … Et puis ce n'est même pas vrai. Ariane elle-même en aurait été désespérée.[74]

Violette suggests then that Jérôme tell his wife the truth about their liaison, regardless of the consequences.

Jérôme,	(avec violence.) Jamais. (Un silence.)
Violette,	(avec douceur.) Pourquoi?
Jérôme.	Je ne te répondrai même pas.
Violette,	(avec une tristesse profonde.) Il n'y a pas d'autre mur entre elle et toi; le jour où il serait tombé …
Jérôme.	C'est faux.
Violette.	Tu sais bien qu'elle te pardonnerait.
Jérôme.	C'est justement l'idée que je ne peux pas supporter. Ce jour-là elle commencerait à me faire horreur … Et nous, nous deux, qu'est-ce nous deviendrions?
Violette.	Il n'y aurait plus de *nous deux.* Il y aurait toi, il y aurait moi … Ou plutôt j'ai tort, il y aurait encore nous deux, il y aura toujours nous deux, mais dans le souvenir.[75]

Ariane comes back to Paris for a visit and calls to see Violette. Ariane had made the acquaintance of Violette's sister at the sanatorium, and uses this as a pretext for the visit. She knows about Jérôme's affair with Violette, although she does not disclose this fact to Violette until later. At their first meeting she asks Violette to give her some lessons in accompanying, during the time she remains in Paris. Violette tries to refuse her request but finally consents to the arrangement. Before this first meeting ends, Ariane tells Violette that she is aware of her liaison with Jérôme.

Violette,	(avec stupeur.) Vous savez?
Ariane.	Depuis quelques jours je n'avais plus aucun doute.
Violette.	Mais Jérôme …
Ariane,	(avec fermeté.) Il ne faut pas encore parler de Jérôme; tout ceic doit rester entre nous.
Violette.	C'est impossible.
Ariane.	Jérôme est un enfant; nous pourrions lui faire beaucoup de mal.
Violette.	Quand il découvrira que vous savez la vérité, je n'imagine pas … le pire peut arriver; il partira, ou bien il se …
Ariane.	Jérôme ne se tuera pas, il ne partira pas, il ne découvrira rien. Tout cela dépend de nous. Vous verrez, vous verrez.[76]

Meanwhile the situation between Jérôme and Violette is becoming unbearable, while Violette, like everyone else who knows Ariane, is much attracted to her:

Ariane.	Il ne faut pas m'admirer; et cet autre sentiment que vous ne parvenez pas à nommer, il ne faut pas vous y abandonner non plus, il me semble. Voyez-vous, il y a d'abord un fait auquel vous ne prenez pas garde. Quand on a traversé les épreuves physiques que j'ai eu à subir pendant des années, il est impossible, je crois, de ne pas considérer la vie … le mot n'est pas exact, de ne pas l'évaluer d'une façon toute nouvelle. Oui, c'est cela, les valeurs sont différentes. je serais tentée de dire que certaines conventions morales ne peuvent être acceptées, ou reconnues que par ceux qui jouissent d'une bonne santé. La maladie, Violette … oh! je ne veux certes pas dire qu'en aucun sens elle soit un privilège, ni qu'elle nous confère la moindre exemption. Mais ce que j'ai pu constater par moi-même, c'est qu'elle modifie notre position par rapport au monde ou à un certain ordre naturel; c'est comme si nous apercevions une face des choses que jusque là nous n'avions même pas soupçonnée. Peut-être une autre dimension du monde.[77]

At last Ariane prepares to go back to the mountains. Jérôme then tells Violette that he will not be put off any longer, he will get a divorce from Ariane and marry her as soon as possible.

Ariane.	Il vous l'a dit sérieusement?
Violette.	Tout à fait sérieusement.
Ariane.	Et qu'avez-vous répondu?
Violette.	J'ai résisté; j'ai cherché à lui démontrer que c'était impossible.
Ariane.	Pourquoi impossible?
Violette.	Et puis ... je ne peux même pas vous expliquer ce qui s'est passé ... Il a certainement cru que je consentirais.
Ariane.	Et en réalité?
Violette,	(très bas.) Je ne sais pas. Peut-être ... cela dépend de vous.[78]

Of course the divorce does not take place. Two months later Jérôme is living at Logny in the mountains with Ariane. He is very unhappy in this environment, and his hatred for his wife becomes more bitter each day. Neither he nor Ariane has had any word from Violette. She had not answered Jérôme's letters nor could he trace her whereabouts. Suddenly one day she comes to their home at Logny. She tells them she is there because her child Monique is ill in a nearby.

The following scene describes the final meeting of these three people:

Violette.	Après m'avoir bourrelée vous voudriez m'endormir ... Mais le simple fait que vous ayez pu suggérer cet odieux arrangement prouve que tout cela est impossible, que tout cela ne doit pas être, ne sera pas. Et vous le savez ... et je me demande si vous n'avez pas tout simplement cherché à m'en convaincre par un long détour perfide ... Comme il aurait mieux valu me dire tout simplement: Je ne veux pas, je refuse. Comme ç'aurait été plus courageux et plus vrai! ... Ou bien est-ce que réellement il a raison? Est-ce que vous appartenez déjà à un

monde que nous ne discernons pas encore? Dites: avez-vous sur nous autres cette avance incompréhensible et que je n'arrive pas à envier? Je ne le crois pas, je ne peux pas le croire; est-ce qu'il n'y a pas dans cette fausse sérénité je ne sais quel mélange sans nom, quelque duperie, quelqu'imposture involontaire? Le savez-vous seulement? Même si l'on pouvait vous contraindre à dire votre plus secrète pensée, serait-ce la vérité? Saurais-je enfin la vérité? (Un long silence.)

Ariane.   Nous ignorons tout de l'avenir. je souhaite du plus profond du coeur que vous n'ayez pas à regretter les mots que vous venez de dire; quoi qu'il arrive, il faudra vous rappeler que je les ai pardonnes.

Violette,   (debout.) Si vous aviez vraiment voulu jouer le jeu, mais pourquoi l'auriez-vous voulu? il n'y avait qu'un moyen, un seul: c'était de vous montrer jalouse, exigeante, mesquine; en un mot c'était de me traiter en rivale. Vous ne pouviez pas vous y refuser sans tricher; vos dés étaient pipés … Oh! mais je vous garde une profonde reconnaissance, Ariane. Vous m'avez enseigné ce que jamais je n'aurais découvert par moi-même—la valeur, la vertu du cynisme.[79]

Jérôme.   Alors tu avoues …

Violette,   (d'un ton changé.) Adieu, Ariane … Oh! je sais … je suis peut-être un monstre d'injustice et d'ingratitude … Puisque la prière vous a été donnée … avec tout le reste … priez quelquefois pour moi—et pour Monique, surtout pour Monique. Parce que si elle ne guérit pas, alors … alors … je ne sais pas … (Elle prend la main d'Ariane, l'embrasse convulsivement et sort.)

(Un long silence.)

Ariane,   (après avoir regardé Jérôme.) Mon Dieu! tout se passe comme si elle avait eu raison! tu n'as pas eu un regard pour elle … Jérôme, est-ce que tu n'as pas de coeur? est-ce que j'ai tué aussi ton coeur? … et

maintenant il ne me sera même plus permis
de mourir.[80]

Has Ariane really triumphed by playing as always "le
beau rôle?" Or has she through her machinations placed
herself in the perpetual hell such as Sartre conceived in *Huis
Clos*? Is Ariane angel or devil? At various points in the play
she fits into one or the other category; she is never the
admixture of both, a human being such as we have learned
to expect from Marcel's best drawn characters. There is
evidence that Marcel himself may be in doubt as to Ariane's
true nature. In writing about this play he says, "Lorsque j'ai
écrit *Le Chemin de Crête*, j'avais une certaine idée du
denouement: mais, arrivé au terme de l'acte trois, je dus
constater que mon personnage central refusait catégori-
quement de se laisser mener où je voulais, et qu'au
dénouement initialement conçu je ne serais en mesure
d'amener qu'un cadavre ... mon personnage ayant ressaisi
l'initiative le lendemain je pus écrire mon dernier acte d'un
seul trait sans une hésitation."[81]
Perhaps more baffling than the character of Ariane is
Marcel's attitude on the subject of illness in this play. His
oft-repeated doctrine that suffering is a privilege which
brings special insights to the sufferer, when put into the
mouth of an Ariane, renders it ironical. She expresses the
ideas that Marcel has seriously presented on this subject but
her actions are those of a completely unfeeling, irresponsible
and vicious person. The effect of this contradiction is
unsettling to a student of Marcel's ideas. Does he suggest
that the exception proves the rule—that Ariane though
wearing all of the trappings of virtue, had never been
touched by her former illness and that even this illness she
has sought to prolong for her own purposes?
In a scene in the final act Ariane says "il n'y a pas de
femmes supérieures—pas plus qu'il n'y a d'hommes
supérieurs? Nous sommes tous des infirmes ... des
mutilés."[82]
If this is an expression of Marcel's sentiments at this point,
he like Lenormand had no hope for humanity. Nowhere in
this play does he make a plea for religious faith nor does he

suggest any other-wordly solution to the problems of his characters.

It is dangerous to believe that an author is using a single one of his characters as his mouthpiece. He is much more likely to use several and thereby to express contradictions in his own soul. But since there is in this play no voice to counteract the powerful voice of Ariane, the evidence is strong that at this particular time, Marcel was experiencing some serious disillusionment.

Edmond Jaloux finds here a resemblance with Ibsen's plays: "On ne saurait lire *Le Chemin de Crête* sans penser à divers drames d'Ibsen où le tragique naît aussi de l'intervention d'une volonté héroïque, exigeant sans raison le sublime de gens qui ne sont pas faits pour le sublime."[83] As for André Bellesort, he admires the character of Ariane without pretending to understand it: "Depuis les drames de Curel, je n'avais rien lu d'aussi fort. Il y a là une femme, Ariane Leprieur qui est certainement une des plus complexes, une des plus énigmatiques figures de notre théâtre."[84]

* * * *

The situation in this play is one of the most interesting of any in Marcel's theatre. He gives us his usual weak man against not one but two strong women: for Violette, had been a resolute person before her meeting with Ariane. She had made her own way in life, refusing easy compromises such as marriage to the wrong man and financial aid in her career, when it was offered from unscrupulous quarters. She truly loved the vacilating Jérôme and was ready to marry him until she met a much stronger woman, Jérôme's wife, Ariane. The latter wasted no time in her effort to break up the relationship between the lovers though she herself did not wish to be a wife to Jérôme. On the surface this seems like a not unusual situation—I don't want him but you can't have him either—but Ariane's need goes deeper than this. She does not want Jérôme, but she needs him to need her and she also needs Violette's admiration. She has a compulsion to be the center of every situation in which she is at all involved, even when she has little interest in the people concerned. In a word Ariane wants to play God.

All of the characters in *Le Chemin de Crête* are drawn with a clarity and a subtlety remarkable even for Marcel who is master of this art. Particularly Ariane, whose personality is so compelling, that from the moment she comes on the scene we are fascinated and alternately attracted and repelled by her; and after the play is finished we remain baffled by her contradictions and her mystery. She possesses a kind of magic which makes her attractive to the reader in the same way that she is to Violette. This attraction is undoubtedly enhanced by the interrogation and the doubt as to her true nature, but magic it is, and as the drama unfolds the fascination and the mystery remain.

Jérôme is a rather typical Marcel man. His weakness, of course, is enhanced by reason of Ariane's strength; but somehow we have greater sympathy for him than for some others of Marcel's male characters. Besides what mere man could possible cope with an Ariane?

We feel sympathy for Violette, caught between her irresistible attraction to Ariane and her love for Jérôme; and most of all for her complete powerlessness to solve her problem after she met Ariane. This weakness is created by Ariane's strength. Earlier in Violette's life she had been able to make serious decisions.

Expressing himself on the subject of Ariane, Marcel said that basically he wished to create a character who would express the feeling of the "unsatisfiedness" he experienced when meeting people whom he did not completely understand.

But could anyone really know or understand Ariane, even her creator? Her ambiguity is rooted in her very being and it seems true that she can no more understnd her motivations than we can. Not understanding her, without the ability to gauge her intentions, we dare not judge her.

Marcel, though he offers neither solution nor hope for Ariane and her victims, does not attempt to impose any moral judgment upon her. As in many others plays of Marcel, the reader is left to share the indecision of the author.

Published in 1936, *Le Fanal* is a one act play written in Paris in three days, December 26th to 28th, 1935. The principal character is a woman who has recently died, the mother of Raymond Chavière. A few years before, she and Raymond's father had been divorced and the father married a much younger woman. Raymond and his mother had lived together in Paris after the divorce and it is here that the father comes to visit his son on the morning of his return to Paris from Biarritz.

Chavière the father, is much shaken by the death of his former wife. He questions Raymond concerning the details of her last illness:

Chavière.	… Je ne te demanderai rien, tu penses bien. Tu comprends, mon petit, tout ça, c'est … Elle ne t'a … j'ose à peine poser la question … elle … il aurait pu se faire … elle ne t'a pas chargé d'une commission pour moi?
Raymond,	(d'une voix neutre.) Aucune.
Chavière,	(à lui-même.) C'est dur …
	....
Raymond.	Tu respires mieux maintenant qu'elle m'a quitté!
Chavière.	Raymond! … J'avais toujours caressé l'espoir qu'un jour, elle et moi, avant de quitter ce monde, nous pourrions avoir l'explication …
Raymond.	Il est probable qu'elle ne s'y serait pas prêtée.
Chavière.	Pourquoi? *(Un silence.)*
Raymond.	D'ailleurs je supposais que vous vous étiez tout dit … à ce moment-là.
Chavière.	Il me semble aujourd'hui que nous n'avons échangé que des paroles fausses … Ta mère, du reste, n'a pas … Elle s'est inclinée … Je n'ai jamais su ce qu'elle pensait … Au fond je crois que je ne l'ai pas connue.[85]

M. Chavière now invites Raymond to make his home with him and his wife Isabelle. Raymond tells his father that he is engaged to be married to Sabine Verdon, a young divorcée.

The father wants to know whether Madame Chavière had
known and approved of the marriage, because he knew that
his former wife had become very pious and would probably
have had objections to a daughter-in-law who had been
divorced. "C'est sans rapports avec la foi qui ne m'a
malheureusement pas été donnée ... Mais ta mère ..."
The visit ends with the father's request to spend a few
moments in the room in which his former wife had died.

However things are not going well with Raymond and
Sabine. Raymond has an attitude of cynicism and bitterness.
Sabine tells him that he must take a vacation; she reminds
him that his mother had wished him to do so and offers to go
away with him:

Raymond,	(avec une âpreté croissante.) ... Es-tu assez contente, assez soulagée, toi auusi! Finies les précautions, les ménagements. On peut s'en donner à présent, téléphoner toutes les heures du jour et de la nuit. C'est la bonne vie qui commence.
Sabine.	Raymond!
Raymond.	La mort, il me semble quelquefois que c'est comme une immense faiblesse dont on abuserait sans pitié, sans vergogne; parce qu'll n'y a plus rien à craindre; plus de querelles à redouter, plus de scènes, plus d'histoires. Rien ne surviendra plus; on peut s'en donner.
Sabine,	(d'un ton changé.) Mais alors, Raymond ... tu me détestes![86]

Raymond next receives a visit from Isabelle, his father's
second wife. She confesses to him that their marriage has
become unbearable and begs Raymond to come to live with
them. She hopes that this might improve the situation. When
Raymond refuses, she tells him that she will then go away
with a man who is in love with her.

Raymond tells Isabelle that he will not marry Sabine and
makes the following confession:

Raymond.	Je dois vous paraître odieux, je le suis en effet. Tout ce que vous m'avez dit était sincère, je n'en doute pas un instant ...

Isabelle, je ne vous juge pas. Je vous plains.
Je vois en ce moment avec une clarté
absolue que votre existence a été triste … Il
y a eu des moments où je vous ai haïe. Je
reconnais à présent distinctement que c'était
absurde, et que c'était mal. Un être tel
qu'était ma mère—un être admirable, oui
c'est vrai Isabelle—est probablement destiné
à creuser beaucoup de souffrance autour de
lui. Je ne sais pas pourquoi il en est ainsi.
C'est un mystère. Vous avez été un des
chemins par lesquels cette souffrance-là s'est
écoulée. Il y en a eu d'autres … Moi-même,
Isabelle. Ce que je vous avoue en ce
moment, je ne l'ai dit à personne. Il y a eu
entre ma mère et moi ce qu'on est convenu
d'appeler une intimité absolue, avec des
moments de merveilleux bonheur. Des
moments … Mais la peur de voir souffrir
par sa faute un être tel que celui-là, l'effort
pour se plier à ses désirs, pour s'ajuster à ses
rêves, la terreur de la décevoir—et quelquefois la rancune, lorsqu'un sacrifice onéreux
semble avoir été jugé naturel—la honte de la
ressentir, cette rancune, les vaines tentatives
pour l'oublier ou pour se la faire pardonner
si par hasard un mot ou un geste l'a trahie
… Ces fiançailles condamnées ont été sans
doute, sans même que je l'aie compris, une
sorte de revanche d'esclave dont je n'ai
même pas joui.[87]

The final scene takes place between Raymond and his
father:

Raymond.	Je voulais justement te proposer … J'ai cru comprendre qu'Isabelle aurait le désir … elle n'a pas osé t'en parler … d'aller passer une quinzaine chez une amie à la campagne; le nom m'échappe …
Chavière.	Quelle idée! elle choisit bien son moment.
Raymond.	Elle avait beaucoup de scrupules à te le demander. Mais cette amie va partir pro-

	chainement pour un grand voyage ... les Indes ou le Japon ...
Chavière.	Elle ne m'en a pas soufflé mot.
Raymond.	Et alors j'ai pensé ... Cela te paraîtra peut-être saugrenu.
Chavière.	Quoi, mon petit?
Raymond.	Pendant qu'Isabelle sera chez son amie ... si toi tu venais habiter ici ...
Chavière,	(avec émotion.) Nous serions tous les deux.
Raymond,	(gravement.) Non, papa, tous les trois, comme autrefois ... comme jamais ...[88]

The principal character in the play, the dead woman, has triumphed. What she could not achieve during her life is now accomplished. Through the pain of her death, all of the irritations which her presence caused have disappeared and she now takes her place in the lives and hearts of the two men.

This short play contains many of the features which are most characteristic of Marcel's theatre. The death theme, in this case expressing the influence of the dead upon the living, is predominant. Its variations touch every character in the play. Madame Chavière, the dead woman, is more alive than any other. She was surely a typical Marcelian woman in her life time. In speaking of her to Raymond, Isabelle, his step-mother, calls her "un être merveilleux" and says of her husband "Il a eu un malheur dans sa vie, c'est d'avoir épousé une femme qui lui était trop supérieure",[89] Her very perfection was perhaps her greatest misfortune. Because of it her marriage failed and her son remained immature, finding the prospect of marriage to anyone of whom his mother disapproved, an impossibility. It is interesting to note that Raymond is able to analyze this condition after his mother's death, though he is unable to correct it.

The question of religion is touched upon several times in connection with Madame Chavière who was a believer. Every other character states categorically that he is entirely without religious faith. It is a fact that among the characters of this play, there are some who are more sympathetically drawn than is Madame Chavière. The effect is that even though we have not known her we feel we may have admired her but would not have loved her.

It is clear that only a first rate playwright could have succeeded within the narrow limits of this play. The character portrayal is true and sure; these people come to life in a few dozen words. The complex relationships between Raymond and his father, between Raymond and his fiancée and his step-mother are movingly drawn and always plausible. But the most vital force in the play is the insistent power of this exigent, dead woman "la lumière au bout de la jetée".[90]

This play was produced at the Comédie Française in 1938 and therefore reviewed by dramatic critics of the time. Maurice Martin du Gard reproaches Marcel for having made it a one act play; this act "étouffe et nous étouffons avec lui". If the play had not been beautifully acted, he adds, it would have seemed almost comic in spite of its funereal atmosphere, for Raymond is nothing but "un jeune idiot", completely ignorant of women, who understands neither his mother nor his fiancée. And then why, Martin du Gard asks, did Madame Chavière divorce her husband if she was a good Catholic?[91]

On the whole it is impossible to disagree with Mr. Martin du Gard's criticism. Raymond is not a very plausible character and certainly not an attractive hero. These imperfections were probably more apparent in the stage production than in the reading of the play, where the character of the dead woman seemed so dominant that the living actors assumed less importance than they would have on the stage.

Henri Bidou says that the principal character in the play does not appear. Marcel, he says, often painted these perfect beings who throw a shadow over the destinies of all whose lives they touched. Such a person was Mme Chavière, beautiful, pious, irreproachable. She is the cause of the sparse events which constitute the play, and after her death, she governs all the tragedy. All of this is suggested rather than explained. "Nous pouvons maintenant mesurer l'art hardi de Gabriel Marcel, qui a confié son drame à ce fantôme."[92]

A year before, Edmond Jaloux describing Raymond's relationship to Sabine, had said "elle lui apparaissait comme le signe de la libération amoureuse; elle n'avait de sens à ses yeux que parce qu'elle s'opposait au seul attachement de sa vie: sa mère".[93]

The last line expresses the heart of the matter. Marcel did not set out to write a Freudian play in which a son's attachment to his mother made every other relationship impossible. This play could be considered an example of the type of complex problem about which Marcel is fond of writing. But actually it *is* a Freudian play, in spite of Marcel's avowed antipathy (i.e., in his criticism of Lenormand) to the use of psychoanalysis in the theatre, and all the more striking because the mother is already dead when her son's relation to her becomes strongest.

La Soif (*Les Coeurs avides*) appeared in the collection "Les Iles". In a note in the 1952 edition of *La Table ronde* Marcel writes: "Pour éviter toute confusion avec l'ouvrage de M. Henri Bernstein de dix ans postérieur qui porte le même titre et sur la demande de M. Lejeune, Directeur du Théâtre du Parc à Bruxelles, qui doit créer la pièce en octobre 1952, j'ai consenti à substituer au titre primitif le titre *Les Coeurs avides*. C'est sous le titre *La Soif* que la pièce a été présentée pour la première fois au public par le club de Provence au Théâtre du Gymnase à Marseiile, le 6 mars, 1949."[94]

Amédée Chartrain, a widower of fifty, married Eveline, a much younger woman who consented to the marriage chiefly because she is fond of his two adult children, a girl Stella, aged twenty and a boy, Arnaud, twenty-four. The family, including his seventy-two year old mother, have little respect for Amédée, who speaks in grandiloquent language with very little meaning. This seems to be his method of covering his insignificance.

The daughter Stella is a confused and unhappy girl. Her mother died in a mental hospital and the girl fears she may have inherited her mental disease. Besides her mother's death was surrounded by mystery; Stella had heard rumours that her mother had attempted to poison her father, and won-

dered what part her father had played in her mother's illness.
To her inquiries Amédée answers:

	Je serai donc aussi explicite que tu me le demandes ... C'est à la suite d'une tentative d'empoisonnement ...
Stella.	Quoi?
Amédée.	Dont j'ai failli être victime—que j'ai été forcé d'exiger l'internement de votre malheureuse mère.
Stella.	Empoi ... elle a voulu t'empoisonner, toi?
Amédée.	J'en ai eu la preuve irréfutable—et elle -même en est convenue ... Je n'ai pas eu d'autre moyen de nous protéger tous trois.[95]

Tormented by these ideas, Stella consents to marry Alain
Puyguerland, a frightened young man, who is convinced that
he will die young in the war he feels imminent. Eveline tried
to dissuade Stella, knowing that the girl does not love Alain,
and feeling that Stella is not in a condition to make an
important decision. But Stella no longer trusts Eveline's
advice and thinks that Eveline opposes the marriage because
Amédée approves of it. Alain tries to persuade Eveline:

	De la pitié, peut-être? Cela ne vaut guère mieux. Non, non, madame, ne protestez pas. Je comprends très bien, je vous assure. Seulement il y a une chose que vous ne saisissez pas ... Voyez-vous, je suis comme beaucoup de mes camarades, je sais quel sort m'attend; je sais que je serai tué dans très peu de temps. Du reste, on me l'a prédit ... Oh! ne souriez pas. Eh bien, moi, je ne crâne pas. J'avoue que c'est une pensée tres difficile à supporter, quand on n'a pas la foi. Très, très difficile ... Alors vous comprenez, si je ne peux pas obtenir la seule chose qui compte pour moi ... ce n'est pas la peine que j'essaye de vivre. J'aime mieux en finir tout de suite—et en somme ce sera une délivrance.
Eveline.	Eh bien! vous êtes en train de me prouver

	combien j'ai raison de penser que ce mariage serait un grand malheur.
Alain.	C'est la vie, madame, qui est un malheur.[96]

In Alain we again have a character obsessed with fear of death, and deprived of the support of religious faith. In a final effort to prevent the marriage, Eveline tells Stella what she believes to be the truth about her mother:

Eveline.	Ta mère n'était pas ce que tu crois. Ce n'était pas une malade ...
Stella.	C'était donc une criminelle?
Eveline.	Pas davantage.
Stella.	Elle a voulu le tuer.
Eveline.	Elle a voulu vivre ... simplement.[97]

At this point, Arnaud, Amédée's son, tells Eveline that he has decided to enter a religious order. Eveline begs him not to do this. Arnaud answers, explaining his position with long metaphysical arguments. It is apparent that Marcel has chosen Arnaud as the character to intervene in order to restore equilibrium to the rest of the characters.

In the final act, Amédée comes home late at night and reports to the family that he has just rescued Alain from an attempted suicide. The following scene ends the play.

Amédée.	Mes pauvres enfants, il y tout de même des instants privilégiés où un ordre se compose, saisissable seulement pour l'oreille la plus délicate et la plus exigeante.
Eveline.	Je comprends à peine ce qui s'est passé; s'est-il seulement passé quelque chose?
	(Amédée s'est assoupi, il murmure: "Pas de la nuit ... aucune importance ...") Eveline le regarde; elle hoche la tête.)
Arnaud,	(avec une pitié profonde, les yeux fixés sur son père.) Encore un peu de temps, et toutes ces phrases dont il s'est enchanté se perdront dans le silence, cette affectation dont il est dupe tombera de lui; il restera là seul, désarmé, sans défense, comme un enfant que le sommeil a terrassé et qui serre encore son jouet contre lui. Devant le vivant qui pérore et gesticule Eveline, si nous savions évoquer

le gisant de demain! ... (Ils le regardent;
Eveline est vaincue par les larmes; elle se
penche et baise Amédée au front comme
peut-être, un jour, plus tard ...)[98]

This is a difficult play to evaluate, because it is weighted
with theological and metaphysical discussion. Though it is
certainly not a thesis play the actual dramatic impact is lost
at times because of the long discussions. The play contains
more intrigue than the majority of Marcel's plays where the
action is mostly psychological. Actually the intrigue in this
play takes place before the curtain rises; the almost cloak
and dagger situation of a suicide in an insane asylum after an
attempt at poisoning is not characteristic of Marcel's writing.

The characters are well drawn, especially that of Amédée
who is presented with all his irritating qualities; though his
son creates sympathy for him when he describes his father's
particular "soif",

Eveline.	Je ne crois pas que ton père soit capable de souffrir—ce que moi j'appelle souffrir.
Arnaud.	Ce que toi ... Il te faut des douleurs estampillées, Eveline. Il y en a d'autres, comme il existe des maladies non reconnues; et ce ne sont pas les moins affreuses. Je crois quant à moi que papa est un homme extrêmement malheureux, d'autant plus malheureux qu'il communique moins avec son mal. L'espèce de soif indistincte qui le dévore, lui-même ne la connaît pas—justement parce qu'elle l'a dévoré.[99]

The daughter Stella, hysterical and intolerant, seems to
bear the deepest scar from the death of her mother and the
mystery surrounding it. Arnaud, her brother, on the contrary
gained from this experience a wisdom far beyond his years
and the incentive to find the way to his own salvation and
that of his family:

Eveline.	D'où te viennent ces lumieres?
Arnaud.	Nous n'en saurons jamais davantage de ce côté de la mort. Sois sûre qu'elle-même n'aurait rien pu expliquer—et lui pas davan-

	tage. Quant à moi, j'ai pris depuis longtemps l'engagement d'accepter cette ignorance.
Eveline.	Vis-à-vis de toi-même?
Arnaud.	Non, c'est un pacte que j'ai conclu.
Eveline.	Avec qui?
Arnaud.	Je n'éprouve pas le besoin de donner un nom à mon ... partenaire; je sais seulement que c'est une présence ... pas une présence humaine ... quelqu'un dont je ne peux pas parler, mais pour qui je suis toi. Il est là. Il veille.
Eveline.	Sur toi?
Arnaud.	Pour moi. Pour nous.[100]

But how does one learn to live with an Amédée? Through the miracle of Arnaud's perception Eveline is able to say the words which are the lesson of the play "je ne juge plus".[101]

Les Coeurs avides, though it contains more discussion of religion than any play since *La Grâce* and *Le Palais de sable*, still fails to be convincing regarding Marcel's religious convictions.

This is the final play in the group which I have called Marcel's first period, these plays were all published between 1914 and 1938. Though they contain varied subject matter, the basic themes are the same—: death and loneliness; and in a majority of the plays there is an allusion, at least, to faith and grace, and some promise of hope.

With practically all rhetoric and didacticism removed from these plays, Marcel's creative art becomes clearer. One sees that this is neither a theatre of observation in the narrow sense nor a theatre of fantasy. Also it would be as difficult to maintain a position that Marcel is dramatist of a "théâtre philosophique" as to accuse him of writing a well-made play.

4—Conflicts resulting from World War II

Le Dard
L'Emissaire
Le Signe de la croix
Rome n'est plus dans Rome

The four plays which follow concern those people, who before, during or after the Second World War, for reasons of race, religion or political conviction, either chose to abandon or were forced to leave their homes.

In *Le Dard* it is Werner the musician who left Germany in protest against the torture and murder of his Jewish accompanist by the Nazis. In the second play *L'Emissaire* we have the sad story of a man who escaped actual death in a concentration camp, but who was returned home completely incapable of participating in family or communal life and who died after a few months. In the next play *Le Signe de la croix* is the tragic history of a Jewish family who considered themselves completely French. Hitler decided otherwise and they were forced to flee from their homes. Their story is the authentic record of many families during this period. *Rome n'est plus dans Rome*, the last and most complex of the four plays, attempts to solve the problem of whether persecuted people should flee in time of crisis or whether they should remain and risk the consequences. Marcel does not believe that an identical solution is valid for everyone.

One idea however, is common to all four of these plays: no matter what the circumstances, the only protection and the only hope for those caught in these cruel dilemmas is strength of the spirit which comes from faith in God. Only here in "l'autre royaume" lies hope; but the problem of man's loneliness remains unsolved, intensified by the conditions created during and after World War II.

Le Dard, published in 1936, although written before the Second World War, is concerned with the same problems Marcel treated later. I feel therefore, that regardless of its date, it belongs with Marcel's post-war plays and I shall discuss it now:

Werner Schnee, an "Aryan" concert singer, has left

Hitler's Germany because his friend and accompanist, Rudolf Schenthal, a Jew, was forced to flee. Rudolf dies in Switzerland as a result of torture he suffered at the hands of the Nazis. Werner has been invited by his old friend Eustache Soreau, whom he had met as a student in Germany, to come to France with his wife, Gisela, as his guest. Werner accepts the invitation but, living in Eustache's home, he finds his friend so changed that he scarcely recognizes him. Eustache has been an ideological Communist, but since his marriage to Béatrice, or more particularly, because of the influence of his father-in-law who is a Senator, Eustache, now successful, has become much less radical. However, his success has brought with it a sense of guilt and Eustache is maladjusted to his environment. Eustache is daily becoming more bitter and cynical.

Several weeks have passed since Werner, the musician, and his wife Gisella, have taken up residence with the Soreaus. The two old friends Werner and Eustache find they disagree on practically every subject, especially politics.

Werner.	Quelquefois je pense que vous … comment on peut dire? que vous inventez des menaces contre vous qui n'existent pas, simplement pour avoir le droit de dire: je suis en danger, je me bats, je me défends.
Eustache.	Vous autres vous ne pouvez rien comprendre à notre situation.
Werner.	Naturellement c'est possible. Les partis en France c'est difficile …
Eustache.	S'il te plaît de croire que l'iniquité sociale n'existe pas …
Werner.	Elle a toujours existé. Probablement elle existera toujours. Mozart et Schubert étaient des pauvres diables; quelquefois ils ne savaient pas s'ils auraient à manger. Ils ne disaient quand même pas: je dois faire de la musique révolutionnaire.
Eustache.	La conscience s'est développée depuis ce temps-là.
Werner.	Quelle conscience?
Eustache.	Il y a des abus que nous ne supportons plus.
Werner.	Pour nous-mêmes ou pour les autres?

Eustache.	Pour les autres. Si ce n'est pas un progrès ...[102]

One day Werner receives an order from the Nazis to return to Germany to give recitals there. He refuses to go and on the strength of this refusal he is threatened with reprisals. When his wife Gisella finds out that he has refused to resume his career in Germany, she leaves him and goes to Rio with a German with whom she had been having a liaison. Werner now lives in a "pension". He describes the environment there and the observations made to him by some of the fellow guests:

Werner.	Mme Brossard m'a dit: quelle chance! vous n'êtes pas communiste! Miss Johnson m'a dit: *luck what! you are not a Jew!* et comme ça ...
Béatrice.	Et alors?
Werner.	Jacques Richemond m'a félicité parce que j'étais un Allemand d'un autre âge, et Mlle Timonnier parce que je n'avais pas de lunettes ... Du reste, j'en mets à présent quand je lis ... Et l'autre jour j'ai chanté une chanson de Schubert: c'était insupportable.[103]

Meanwhile Eustache is having an affair with his Communist friend Gertrude. It is obvious that he does not love her. Béatrice, who knows what is going on, finally tells her husband she will give him a divorce, but Werner tells her:

(fortement.) Vous ne pouvez pas l'abandonner. Il faut vous rappeler toujours que vous êtes la femme d'un pauvre ... La pauvreté n'est pas le manque d'argent, il a eu le succès: il est resté pauvre, toujours plus pauvre; il ne guérira sans doute jamais de sa pauvreté. C'est le plus grand mal de notre temps, il se répand comme une peste; on n'a pas encore trouvé de médecin pour le soigner. On ne sait même pas le reconnaître. L'artiste y échappera sans doute, même s'il ne mange pas à sa faim. Et aussi le fidèle qui a la prière ... Tous les autres sont menacés.[104]

Werner himself has decided to go back to Germany, not to give concerts but to share the fate of the doomed people there.

Béatrice,	(passionnément.) Mais, Werner, s'ils vous fusillent?
Werner,	(simplement.) Ce n'est pas impossible, mais je ne pense pas du tout ... Je me mets simplement à la disposition.
Béatrice.	De qui, Werner? de quoi? de la cause? de la révolution?
Werner.	La cause ne m'intéresse pas; les hommes m'intéressent ...[105]

The play ends with the following dialogue:

Werner.	Les léproseries vont se multiplier sur la terre, je le crains. Ce sera une grâce réservée à très peu d'y vivre en sachant qu'on vit parmi les lépreux, et sans les prendre en horreur. Plus encore qu'une grâce. Comment dites-vous? *viaticum* ... un viatique.
Béatrice.	Je ne suis pas assez brave, Werner, je vous assure.
Werner.	Vous penserez à moi comme je pense à Rudolf. Plus tard je vous habiterai comme Rudolf m'habite ... Et vous vous rappellerez alors ce que je vous ai dit il y a quelques semaines: s'il n'y avait que les vivants, Béatrice ...[106]

In analyzing the play it becomes evident that the two main characters, Werner and Eustache, apparently so different in character, are both suffering from a guilt complex. "Le Dard" which pierced and poisoned Eustache is very different from the cross which Werner feels compelled to bear. Eustache's guilt springs from a personal conflict; he deserted a cause to which he had committed himself. Certainly the presence of Werner hastened the collapse of Eustache's moral character. The comparison between Eustache's present life and the sacrifice that Werner had made were too great a strain on his conscience. Werner's guilt is the universal guilt felt by those who escape a holocaust through no particular merit of their own. Werner is one of those who is not content to protest or merely to aid the stricken, but who must share the pain. It is the Christ symbol which Marcel offers us.

The political implications of the play are very important. While presenting the Nazi horror, Marcel, at the same time shows the beginning of the bankruptcy of Communist ideology as it appeared to him in 1936. To be sure not all Communist adherents were as vulgar as a Gertrude or as unstable as an Eustache, but the process of disillusionment had begun to set in at that time among certain groups.

Werner and his wife are the first characters of a large company of displaced people whom Marcel presents in these four plays. He is primarily interested in the effect produced by the persecutions of Nazism and Communism; but we shall also recognize the themes of "death" and "loneliness" which were predominant in the preceding plays. In this play it was the death of the Jew Rudolph which motivated the action of Werner. The theme of "loneliness" is beautifully expressed by Béatrice: "J'ai souvent remarqué que dans la vie ce qu'il y a de plus affreux ne mène jamais au drame. Le pire, c'est ce qui ne débouche nulle part. Je ne sais pas, c'est comme ces rues qui se perdent dans des terrains vagues, au bord des grandes villes. Il me semble quelquefois que nos vies sont pareilles à ces avenues à peine construites, où personne ne passe, et qui portent le nom d'on ne sait quel conseiller municipal ..."[107]

Again in this play Marcel shows the great importance of music in his life. His main character is a concert singer who says "si la musique devient plus pauvre, alors la vie aussi diminue, elle devient mesquine. Sans la musique on ne vit plus, on vivote ... est-ce qu'on dit ça en français?"[108]

But the most important message of the play is contained in the lines "Ce sera une grâce réservée à très peu d'y vivre en sachant qu'on vit parmi les lépreux, et sans les prendre en horreur".[109]

The privileged of mankind must share their gifts with the less fortunate. It is the specially endowed and the dead heroes and the saints who have set the example; and if we follow them peace may come to remove despair from the hearts of men.

Edmond Jaloux judges this play thus: "Dans *Le Dard* on trouvera exprimés par des personnages bouffons tous les lieux communs politiques qu'on entend chaque jour. Il faut être reconnaisant à Gabriel Marcel de nous emporter au dela de ces professions de foi électorales. Il faut l'admirer d'oser mettre en lumière les drames qui relèvent de la condition humaine et non des positions des partis. Cela lui permettra de franchir les limites des modes de notre temps".[110]

Jaloux has seen the play's greatest merit. Marcel in treating problems created by certain temporary conditions as essentially human problems, "qui relèvent de la condition humaine", has succeeded in giving the play a durable and permanent interest.

Marcel published his next two plays *L'Emissaire* and *Le Signe de la croix* under the title *Vers un autre royaume* with the sub-title "Deux Drames des années noires". They appeared in 1949 in one volume followed by a postface by the author.

> Les deux drames qui se trouvent réunis dans ce volume portent sur quelques-uns des problèmes les plus brûlants qui se posent à nous aujourd'hui, de ceux qu'il est le moins possible d'éluder.
>
> Ce qui s'est imposé à moi au cours de ces terribles années, et ce que je n'avais pas encore aperçu distinctement en 1938, c'est que la persécution transforme tous les rapports, qu'elle crée un lien, et qu'en refusant de reconnaître ce lien on risque de glisser vers la trahison.
>
> Il en est de même pour *L'Emissaire*. La pièce est tournée vers les non fanatiques, vers ceux qui supportent de regarder en face une réalité historique infiniment complexe et douloureuse—et qui ne se laisse pas simplifier comme certains l'ont cru. Ce sera toujours pour moi un sujet de surprise et de scandale que des chrétiens—je dis des chrétiens—aient pu former sur les événéments de 40-44 des jugements unilatéraux, et au nom de ces jugements porter des condamnations dont beaucoup sont demeurées jusqu'ici sans appel.[111]

The action of *L'Emissaire* takes place in the home of the Ferrier family in the vicinity of Paris, in February 1945. Clément Ferrier has just been sent home after sixteen months in the concentration camp of Schlackwitz in Polish Silesia. He is in a deplorable physical condition and his doctor has forbidden him to see any visitors except his immediate family. In the household are his wife Mathilde, two daughters, Anne-Marie Sérol, her husband, Bertrand, and Sylvie, engaged to marry Antoine Sorgue.

The only suspense in this play is connected with the conditions under which Clément Ferrier, "L'Emissaire", has been permitted to leave a concentration camp. In the short period of time that he remains alive after his return home, Clément fails to establish any normal relations with his family. He never once refers to his life in the camp or to the circumstances of his leaving it. The family does not attempt to force him to speak.

Antoine Sorgue, the fiance of Sylvie, suspects that Clément may have been returned to accomplish some evil design of the Germans.

Antoine.	Réfléchissez. Vous demandez quel intérêt l'ennemi pouvait avoir à libérer votre père dans des conditions telles qu'on pût croire à son évasion. Il pouvait s'agir pour eux tout simplement de renvoyer ici un témoin de scènes atroces, qui par son attitude, et même par son silence, contribuerait à répandre autour de lui l'angoisse et la terreur et deviendrait ainsi un foyer de démoralisation. Mais la manoeuvre ne pouvait réussir qu'à condition de demeurer insoupçonnée; il fallait donc que ce témoin parût s'être libéré lui-même contre la volonté formelle de ses bourreaux ...
Bertrand.	Cela me paraît tiré par les cheveux.
Roger.	Il faut reconnaître qu'avec eux tout est possible; l'art de manipuler le moral n'a jamais été poussé aussi loin.
Anne-Marie,	(à Antoine). Vous iriez donc jusqu'à prétendre que le silence de mon père est un silence commandé?
Antoine.	Pas nécessairement, mais il peut très bien être le résultat d'une suggestion exercée méthodiquement sur lui pendant les semaines

> qui ont précédé son départ. Comme il est
> possible aussi qu'il traduise simplement un
> état d'attrition morale.[112]

Clément dies after a few weeks without ever having shown any happiness in being at home with his family. The family feels that it was not really he who had returned; that in fact the real Clément had died in the concentration camp. The mystery of his discharge from camp is cleared by a letter received by the family after his death from a fellow prisoner in the concentration camp who had been granted his freedom, and who had insisted that Ferrier be freed in his place.

Marcel has shown us a pathetic picture and certainly has given a true account of what happened in many cases during the war. More often, however, the only thing the Nazis returned to families was a box of ashes and that was before the furnaces of Dachau and other places destroyed the family as a whole.

But Gabriel Marcel's primary purpose in writing this play was not to arouse sympathy for those people, such as Clément, who were doomed to destruction by forces outside of France. *L'Emissaire* is concerned with a problem which even up to the present time, has not been so widely discussed—the effect of France's Resistance Movement upon Frenchmen themselves. Marcel recognizes that people, because of differences of character and emotional stability, do not all react to danger in the same way. The war and the occupation produced not only a Resistance Movement but also traitors and collaborators. It also produced another group—those people who were neither traitors nor collaborators but were not so constituted as to be able to do heroic or violent acts. Some of these joined the movement and left it and others never became a part of it.

Marcel presents us with a character representing each group. Bertrand, the son-in-law of the Ferriers, is a Resistance man par excellence. Sylvie, the Ferrier's daughter has been in the movement but was forced to leave it for physical and emotional reasons. Antoine Sorgue, her fiancé, had fought in the war, been wounded and returned home, but failed to join the Resistance and was therefore suspect. Roland Garmoy, the son of a friend of Madame Ferrier was a collaborationist who hanged himself when he was discovered and his act caused his mother to commit suicide.

But Marcel endeavors to show in this play that however high the purpose and great the accomplishment of the Resistance Movement, it was also a divisive force in France. Loyal Frenchmen misjudged the motives and activities of other loyal Frenchmen. Thus Bertrand, the Resistance man, says of Antoine, the wounded soldier:

	Il est de ceux qui se sont imaginés ou qui ont affecté de croire—je dis affecté parceque cette position était intenable pour un homme de bonne foi.
Antoine.	Ce serait tout de même un peu trop simple si d'un côté il y avait la sagesse, la vérité, l'héroïsme, la foi … et de l'autre, le cynisme, la lâcheté, la trahison …
Sylvie.	le courage consistant?
Antoine.	d'abord à nous accepter, et à nous exprimer par des actes qui soient nous-mêmes.
Sylvie.	Je ne me reconnais plus. Je ne sais plus où je suis, qui je suis … et je me demande si les trois quarts des Français ne sont pas au même point que moi.[113]

And Marcel himself says in the Postface to the play:

Certains objecteront probablement que Bertrand, l'homme de la résistance, a moins de relief humainement et dramatiquement qu'Antoine qui, lui, n'a pas *résisté*. La raison de ce fait est très simple: c'est que la résistance ne peut guère se penser au passé sans changer de nature. L'ancien résistant, comme l'ancien combattant, risque toujours de devenir un personnage problématique, car on ne résiste et on ne combat qu'au présent. Bertrand, qui est un être d'une grande droiture et même d'une veritable noblesse a conscience de cette difficulté, de ce piège; en même temps il ne peut aucunement renier ses actions passées,—je dirais même personnellement qu'il n'en a pas le droit,—mais comment ne verrait-il pas qu'elles ont porté ailleurs bien des fruits empoisonnés? Cette situation crée nécessairement chez lui une certaine contrainte; il n'a pas mauvaise conscience, mais comment serait-il à son aise dans un monde où l'action à laquelle il a participé de tout son être a dégénéré après coup en une comédie sinistre?[114]

Sylvie suffered greatly because a friend of hers, Noémie Vitrel, a member of the Resistance, was arrested by the Nazis and sent to Bischoffsbruck. The mission during which Noémie was arrested had been intended for Sylvie to carry out. At this point Sylvie had found it impossible to remain in the movement. Now Noémie, free and back in France has joined a group in blackmailing those who did not work with them. Noémie has accused Sylvie of informing upon her to the Nazis. Sylvie feels she can never prove her innocence because she cannot establish the fact that she had not written an anonymous letter. When Sylvie inquires the reason for this blackmail, she is told by an ex-resistant that it is possible Noémie and other Communists are trying to collect money for the widows of their comrades, "Ce qui confond c'est que tant d'êtres soient revenus de ces bagnes sans haine, sans esprit de vengeance. Les autres, Noémie et ses semblables, nous devons les comprehendre et n'avons pas à les juger"[115]

Marcel himself writes in the Postface the following words on this subject:

Le chantage auquel Noémie semble vouloir se livrer contre Sylvie peut et doit paraître assez odieux; et cependant, si je suis tout à fait équitable, je suis obligé de reconnaître que de son point de vue même, il n'est pas tout à fait sans excuses. Elle est devenue une fanatique, elle a des morts à venger, comment ne s'attribuerait-elle pas des droits, pour les victimes, sur l'argent de ceux qui, d'après elle, n'ont pas souffert et ont manqué de courage à l'heure décisive? Dans la perspective de Noémie tout cela est parfaitement soutenable; chose étrange, on ne pourrait la condamner que d'un point de vue transcendant, mais la transcendance vivante exclut tout jugement.[116]

Having delivered the real thesis of the play and having made a plea for justice and tolerance for the people of the Resistance and the non-resistants, Marcel considers once more the case of Clément Ferrier, the emissary and the play ends thus:

Sylvie.   Mon père ... il me semble à présent que

j'entrevois le sens de ce retour humainement
incompréhensible ... Le retour ambigu de ce
mort vivant, de ce responsable irresponsable
pour lequel un autre s'est sacrifié, et c'est
l'autre qui survit ... Oui. C'est à la lumière
de cette ambiguité que tout finit par
s'éclairer, précisément par ce qu'elle décon-
certe à l'infini tout jugement ... Qui som-
mes-nous pour juger serait-ce nous mêmes?
(Un long silence. Tous trois s'absorbent dans
une méditation profonde.)[117]

From the standpoint of drama, this is really not a good
play. However it is important in Marcel's theatre, because it
presents an interesting problem that had heretofore received
little attention. Marcel is writing about a group of
emotionally displaced persons. Their position was not quite
as dramatically tragic as those of the physically displaced
who were torn away from their homes and tortured by an
alien enemy; but it was none the less heart-breaking for a
loyal Frenchman to be misjudged and misunderstood by his
fellow citizens. These peoples' lives were completely dislocated by the war and by a situation in which they had had
no previous experience to guide their conduct. How can they
be judged according to the usual human standards?

One cannot discuss *L'Emissaire*, however, without com-
paring it with a drama witten on more or less the same
subject a few years before by Armand Salacrou: *Les Nuits
de la colère*. This play was produced for the first time on
December 12, 1946, by the Madeleine Renaud—Jean Louis
Barrault Company at the Marigny Theatre. Salacrou calls his
play "un documentaire sur l'occupation, un procès-verbal."
It is a drama of the Resistance which takes place in Chartres
in June 1944, in which a Frenchman delivers his best friend
into the hands of the enemy.

Using the retrospective method, Salacrou manages to
create the atmosphere of eye-witness reporting. The delicate
psychological situation is handled with great feeling, and
even where the satire is bitter, there is sympathetic understanding of the problem.

Bernard Bazière of Chartres, who delivered his friend to

the Germans on the insistence of his wife, Pierrette, is neither a coward nor a traitor; he does not even lack great love of his country. He is a man whose only desire is to live peacefully; he has a horror of war, this war, all wars. His ideal is the Cathedral of Chartres, its beauty, its calm, its eternity. When the lives of his wife and children are menaced by the presence of his friend Jean Cordeau in their home, he succumbs to his wife's plea that his friend be forced to leave in order to avoid suspicion of taking part in the blowing up of an enemy supply train. Jean, a leader in the Resistance is also a peaceful man, but he believes that peace has to be fought for, and so he has joined other peace-loving men in derailing trains carrying supplies to the Germans.

Jean, in speaking with his companions uses words expressing the same idea as do the characters of Gabriel Marcel—the oft-repeated cry of loneliness: "Rivoire, sais-tu ce qui m'a fait le plus mal? ... Me sentire si seul ... D'abord la Résistance de quoi? ... Moi, un terroriste! ... Mais réflechissez, je suis un intellectuel, ingénieur, chimiste" "... Dans cette nuit qui n'en finit pas, il n'y a d'espoir que dans la lutte ... Plutôt mourir debout que vivre à genoux." His friend then asks "Et quand tu seras mort debout, que pourras tu encore espérer?" Jean: "Que mes enfants vivront libres."

These are words of an idealist who can bear the idea of war and killing because he can envisage a future when war will be abolished, but there were other groups, loyal Frenchmen, who could not subscribe to this idea.

Both Salacrou and Marcel, recognizing that war changes all relationships and that the Resistance Movement was a divisive force among Frenchmen, plead for understanding of the non-Resistant who is neither a traitor nor a collaborationist. Both writers saw loyal Frenchmen judging other loyal Frenchmen—differences in basic characteristics causing different reactions in an extraordinary and tragic situation.

While Salacrou's play expresses hope that war can be abolished, Marcel characteristically stresses the human tragedy which stems from the impossibility of one human being to communicate with another or even totally to understand himself. In this play we see people who carry within themselves the extreme contradictions inherent in human beings. It is difficult to tell truth from falsehood, right from wrong. In this situation how can one judge the actions of another?

Both *Les Nuits de la colère* and *L'Emissaire* deal with a complex problem which did not arise until the Second World War and as such they are important additions to the contemporary theatre.

Salacrou's play is a better one than Marcel's. The main reason for this is that Marcel attempted to portray two situations in his play, one, the pitiful state of a man returned from a concentration camp and the effect of his return upon him and his family, and two, how certain groups of Frenchmen reacted to the Resistance movement. These are two completely different themes, and need to be treated in separate plays. The situation of the returned prisoner and his relation to his family and theirs to him contains enough material for one, first-rate psychological drama. By adding to this a portrayal of the effect of the Resistance movement on the psychology of individuals, he weakened the first theme.

When Marcel attempted his second theme—the Resistance—his approach was too intellectual and too loquacious. On the other hand, Salacrou, placing his characters in a situation where they experience one night of terror, makes the most of all the possibilities of action both real and psychological.

In his review of *Les Nuits de la colère* in the *Revue Théâtrale* Marcel admires in it the point he will try to make apparent in *L'Emissaire*: that is to say the difficulty of judging peoples' actions in circumstances as tragic as the occupation and the Resistance:

> ... je dois dire que la pièce me paraît remarquable et que l'auteur n'a probablement rien fait de supérieur à la deuxième partie, c'est-à-dire aux scènes qui préparent la trahison—cette trahison que ses auteurs n'auront même pas la force ou le courage de reconnaître pour ce qu'elle est. Il y a là, d'ailleurs, probablement une indication extrêmement profonde: combien de traîtres ont eu vraiment conscience d'être des traîtres? Le vocable trahison ne correspond-il pas à une image infiniment simplifiée de quelque chose qui se présente à l'agent comme un

enchevêtrement inextricable de situations et de motifs? La vérité
est que, dans les époques paisibles, Bernard et Pierrette seraient,
selon toute vraisemblance, restés ce que nous appelons des
honnêtes gens; ce sont des gens qui ne demandaient qu'à vivre
tranquillement et, dans des conditions d'existence normale, ils
auraient pu réaliser cet idéal médiocre certes, mais non point
condamnable, sans avoir à enfreindre aucune obligation morale
précise. Mais, malheureusement pour eux, ils se sont trouvés
appelés à vivre en un temps où cette tranquillité ne pouvait être
obtenue qu'au prix des actes les plus déshonorants; la situation
dans laquelle ils se trouvent est de celles qui contraignent un
être à tomber bien au-dessous de son propre niveau, ou à
s'élever infiniment au-dessus; mais ils sont incapables d'admettre
ou de reconnaître la nécessité de cette option. D'autant—et ceci
est marqué dans *Les Nuits de la colère* avec la plus grande
force—que leur univers mental est irréductible à celui auquel
appartiennent les résistants, ceux qu'ils appellent des fous ou des
terroristes. Il est à peu près certain que, jusqu'au bout, des êtres
comme ceux-là s'apparaîtront à eux-mêmes comme les victimes
d'une fatalité monstrueuse, non point à aucun degré comme des
coupables.[118]

Marcel sees in Salacrou's play what he, no doubt, wants
L'Emissaire to be: a plea for understanding of Frenchmen by
Frenchmen:

Le plus grand mérite de la pièce de M. Salacrou consiste
peut-être en ce qu'elle favorise cette compréhension et apparaît
ainsi comme une oeuvre de contre-propagande: je vise bien
entendu par là non pas une propagande opposée à une propagande, mais le refus actif de participer à une action dirigée en
fait, quelles que soient ses modalités, contre les valeurs sans
lesquelles il ne peut exister ni de pensée, ni d'art dignes de ce
nom.[119]

L'Univers Concentrationnaire by David Rousset, 1945,
would be valuable reading as a preface to Marcel's *L'Emissaire*. Having read Mr. Rousset's description of Buchenwald,
Neuengamme and other camps, one could well understand
the state of mind and body of the "Emissaire" when he was
returned to his home.

Le Signe de la croix

Nul ne peut contester que le problème d'Israël ait pris un regain d'actualité dramatique. Ici, d'après ce qu'on m'affirme, les conversions se multiplient et ailleurs un judaïsme et forcené menace de dégénérer en un nouveau nazisme aussi indéfendable que l'autre. Entre ces deux extrêmes il demeure cependant des hommes de bonne foi, de bonne volonté, et c'est à eux que s'adresse cet ouvrage.[120]

The first act was written in 1938, the major part of the second in 1942 and the third in 1945. Marcel says: "Je n'ai à vrai rien cru devoir changer aux scènes composeés il y a plus de dix ans, car ce tableau, pour cruel qu'il puisse sembler, continue à me sembler exact."[121]

Acts I and II take place in the summer of 1938 at Garches; the third act in 1942 in a town in the Unoccupied Zone. Simon Bernauer, his wife Pauline, and their three sons, David, Jean-Paul and Henri, live in a large villa that Pauline and her brother Léon have inherited from their parents. They have as their guest tante Léna, a pious Jewess, who has come as a refugee from Vienna.

When the play begins, Simon's wife Pauline has just had a message that her brother, a doctor, will no longer be permitted to treat patients at the hospital. This is the result of a ruling in certain Paris hospitals, to exclude Jewish doctors from their staffs. Simon tells tante Léna that his brother-in-law, the doctor, has contributed much to medicine, in the way of personal research, is a good clinician, and a credit to the staff of any good hospital. He adds however that in spite of boasts of some Jews, arising from their loyalty to their co-religionists, not all Jewish doctors are of the excellent calibre of his brother-in-law.

	Mais ni mon beau-frère, ni Pauline n'en conviendront jamais. Et voyez-vous, tante Léna, c'est là que le drame commence.
Tante Léna.	Le drame?
Simon.	Oui … Les nôtres se tiennent; l'un n'est pas plutôt arrivé a l'échelon supérieur qu'il se retourne vers les camarades pour leur tendre la main.
Tante Léna,	(sans conviction.) N'est-ce pas l'esprit d'entre-aide? Est-ce que ce n'est pas beau?
Simon.	Ce qui est inquiétant, c'est qu'il y a là une

Tante Léna.

contradiction qu'ils ne reconnaîtront jamais. Ils veulent être considérés comme des Français pareils à tous les autres, et en même temps ils se traitent entre eux comme les membres d'une franc-maçonnerie. Vous dites: ils veulent? Est-ce que vous vous mettez à part?[122]

Marcel now tells Simon Bernauer's tragic story which is the story of many Jews living in the free world at this period. Simon is a Jew without religious affiliation of any kind. He rejects the theory of racism and denies even that ties exist between Jews. His older son David challenges his father's ideas and Simon answers him,

(s'emportant.) Alors je suis condamné à penser, à sentir en juif? Tu prétends me parquer dans une certaine façon de juger? dans une espèce de ghetto mental? Tu ne comprends pas que c'est du racisme, justement, le plus niais, le plus borné qui soit? Et que par là, malheureux, tu donnes des armes à nos adversaires. Tu justifies par avance leurs assertions les plus choquantes, les plus dangereuses. Oh! d'ailleurs, j'ai souvent pensé que l'idée raciste, c'etaient les Juifs qui l'avaient lancée dans le monde.[123]

Simon's younger son, Jean-Paul, is about to be baptised a Protestant, while every day Pauline becomes more alarmed at what she considers to be further signs of anti-Semitism in France.

Pauline.

Nous sommes une communauté, plus on nous persécutera, plus nous serons tenus de le sentir et de l'affirmer.

Simon.

Nous ne sommes pas persécutés.

Pauline.

La question existe, tu l'avoues.

Simon.

Par votre faute; parce que vous jouez délibérement sur les deux tableaux. Vous voulez profiter de tous les avantages que vous confère votre nationalité, mais en même temps vous ne pouvez vous résoudre à désserrer entre vous ce lien fatal dont on ne

> sait plus si c'est un lien de croyance, de race
> ou de tradition. Pourquoi? peut-être au fond
> parce que vous aimez la puissance, les
> privilèges, parce que vous gardez le besoin
> de vous sentir élus, alors même que vous
> avez cessé depuis longtemps de croire en un
> Dieu qui vous aurait choisis. Cette élection a
> dégénéré. Ce n'est plus que la volonté tenace
> de vous imposer en maîtres au peuple qui a
> bien voulu vous accueillir comme ses
> enfants.[124]

Pauline's brother, the doctor, is offered a position in an
American hospital and Pauline urges him to accept it. It is
now 1942 and the Bernauers, Simon, Pauline, their little
daughter and tante Léna are living in a town in the
unoccupied zone of Southern France. The two boys David
and Jean-Paul have remained in Paris. The family has not
been molested but Pauline is convinced that if the war
continues for any length of time, all Jews must emigrate
across the sea or face extermination. One day Jean-Paul
arrives from Paris with the news that his brother David has
been arrested. Wearing his yellow star, he went to a concert.
Admission to any place of public entertainment was forbidden to Jews and David was immediately apprehended,
struck by a German officer and dragged from the hall.
Simon's first reaction on hearing the news was one of pride
in his son's courage:

> Cette témérité, cette folie ... Et pourtant,
> saviez-vous, tante Léna, je suis fier de lui.
> Cet enfant qui a été à la mort parce qu'il ne
> reconnaissait pas à des brutes le droit, de le
> priver de musique ... Tante Léna! Mais
> c'est horrible! ... Mais quel sens a tout cela?
> Et Jean-Paul! Moi qui ai tant souhaité que
> mes enfants soient chrétiens, cette conver-
> sion-là ne m'inspire pas confiance ... Je ne
> sais pas ... C'est une fuite ...[125]

A short time later the family is notified that David is dead.

Simon,   (douloureusement.) Nous aurons mis à l'abri

	notre piano à queue, notre Vuillard, notre argenterie ... et nous n'aurons pas trouvé le moyen de sauver notre enfant ...
Tante Léna.	Simon! Simon! Sauver un être ce n'est pas le mettre à l'abri. Il n'y a pas de garde-meuble pour les hommes, vous le savez bien.[126]

The Bernauer family is now warned to leave the country. If a landing were to occur anywhere in France, the Germans would occupy the whole country and Jews would be deported and exterminated. Simon refuses to leave but urges Pauline to take the two children to America where her brother has offered them a home. Tante Léna will not emigrate and, fearing that Simon would refuse to leave her, has made contact with a certain Abbé Schweigsam, who is trying to arrange to have her accepted in a refuge home for Jews. This home is being organized by the Catholic Church with support from the Vatican, but the rule under which the refuge is organized provides only for French Jews, and tante Léna is not a French citizen. The good Abbé wishes her to come to live in his house as a relative.

As Simon expected, tante Léna refuses the Abbé's generosity saying she is old and weak and quite prepared to die, and that certainly the French and young people must have priority.

The Abbé is surprised when Simon tells him that he will not go to America with his family, "Mais il est normal qu'un mari, un père ..."[127] Simon answers that there is no longer any meaning to the word normal and requests permission to make a statement to the Abbé which will be in the nature of a confession:

> Il n'y a pas de rabbin ici, monsieur l'Abbé, et d'ailleurs les rabbins ne sont pas des confesseurs ... D'autre part, je ne suis pas un Juif croyant. Mes parents, ma femme, moi, nous étions des gens complètement détachés ... Oh! je le dis sans aucune fierté, bien au contraire, plutôt avec confusion ... Je crois apercevoir aujourd'hui que ces calamités incroyables qui s'abattent une fois de plus sur ...

Abbé Schweigsam.	Sur vos malheureux frères …
Simon.	Hélas! jusqu'à ces derniers mois je ne les ai pas regardés comme mes frères, je contestais qu'il y eût entre eux et moi plus qu'un lien humain ordinaire, je ne me sentais pas plus près d'un juif de Galicie que d'un nègre ou d'un hindou. Encore maintenant, je ne le puis pas, et je ne regrette pas que ce sentiment me soit étranger, car il me semble qu'il mène au racisme, cette monstruosité. Mais une conviction s'est abattue sur moi comme un poids. Surtout depuis que j'ai reçu cette affreuse nouvelle: c'est que la persécution … je ne sais comment m'exprimer. J'ai une telle horreur des phrases, monsieur l'Abbé … Dès le moment où un juif de Galicie qu'en temps ordinaire j'aurais évité—peut-être pas méprisé, mais évité— … Du moment qu'il vit dans ce pays et qu'il est pérsécuté, je n'ai plus le droit de me détourner de lui, il a reçu comme un sacrement et je dois le partager comme on partage le pain bénit … Ce qu'il y a de plus étrange c'est que je ne comprends pas moi-même ce que je vous dis, pourtant je sais qu'il en est ainsi. Ou bien estimez-vous que je cède à un vertige à la suite de cet événément horrible? Et voyez-vous, monsieur l'Abbé, il me semble que ma tante pour qui j'ai une tendresse filiale, m'a été envoyée comme un ange … je veux dire un messager porteur d'un ordre qu'elle même ignore, car elle ne cesse de me supplier de partir avec les miens. Pourtant c'est elle, c'est sa présence.[128]

And Simon continues:

> … N'ai-je pas le droit de penser que ces
> événements ont un sens et qu'il m'appartient
> de le découvrir? que tante Léna m'a été
> donnée pour éclairer ma route. Pourquoi
> certains êtres ne seraient-ils pas placés sur
> notre chemin comme des lumières?

Abbé Schweigsam.	Et vous dites que vous n'avez pas la foi!
Simon.	Je ne sais pas ce que je crois. La grande différence entre moi et beaucoup d'autres que je connais, c'est que j'ai compris que je ne le sais pas. Me trompé-je en pensant que cette foi qui peut-être m'habite deviendra pour moi-même plus distincte lorsque j'aurai obéi ...

....

Abbé Schweigsam,	(avec une profonde émotion.) Mais vous êtes chrétien!
Simon.	Je n'ai en tout cas qu'un seul moyen de me le prouver à moi-même, c'est de me rendre solidaire de la souffrance des plus juifs parmi les Juifs, de ceux qu'on a livrés sans pitié à l'horreur ... [129]

....

Tante Léna.	Mais alors, Simon, si ce n'est pas à cause de moi que vous restez avec moi, s'il y a une autre raison beaucoup plus haute pour que vous partagiez mon sort, alors je ne m'oppose plus ... seulement faites attention, moi je ne suis pas chrétienne ... Je ne suis pas sûre que vous ayez le droit de laisser partir les autres sans vous. Peut-être voyez-vous une lumière que je n'aperçois pas encore ...
Simon,	(avec tendresse.) Et cependant, tante Léna, cette lumière c'est en vous et autour de vous qu'elle n'a cessé de briller depuis que nous nous sommes rencontrés.[130]

Le Signe de la croix, Marcel told us was resented in many quarters in Paris and has never been played. The attack on the separatist tendencies of large groups of Jews, coming at a time when the consciousness of Jewish identification was intensified by the Nazi holocaust which had destroyed six million Jews, was naturally resented. However Jewish group consciousness is a fact. The events in the Middle East and elsewhere in the last ten years have shown that group consciousness can become fanaticism; it is possible that it could destroy a people and endanger the peace of the world.

Marcel's play could have been a warning to Jews but they
were unwilling and unready to heed it.

From the standpoint of drama, this is a far better play
than *L'Emissaire*. The characters are real people and the
conflicts in their souls are vividly portrayed as is the tragedy
of the events in which they are caught up.

Marcel presents an important Jewish and human problem,
and at the same time produces drama of high quality. It is in
this respect that *L'Emissaire* somehow fails. The message
comes through but the sense of real drama is lacking. *Le
Signe de la croix* in spite of its philosophical content is as
good a play for example as the *Chapelle ardente*.

Some of the most important characteristics of Marcel's
drama are present in this play. The Death Theme, in this
case the murder of Simon's son David, plus the fact that
Jews were dying in concentration camps and furnaces,
transformed Simon's thinking and emotional response
toward his fellow Jews.

Theme Two, is shown in lack of communication or
sympathetic understanding between Simon and Pauline. But
utter loneliness is missing for almost the first time in any
play of Marcel's, because of the beautiful relationship
between Simon and tante Léna.

Faith plays a major role in the final scenes of the play.
Simon may not be Marcel's spokesman but his words "Je ne
sais pas ce que je crois. La grande différence entre moi et
beaucoup d'autres que je connais, c'est que j'ai compris que
je ne le sais pas",[131] carry such power that it is difficult to
believe that the voice of Marcel is not speaking; a Marcel not
yet committed to a dogmatic faith.

Also significant are Simon's words "Tante Léna m'a été
donnée pour éclairer ma route". Tante Léna is not the usual
intermediary but a Jewess who warns Simon saying
"seulement faites attention, moi je ne suis pas Chrétienne":[132]

Judging his play in the Postface, Marcel says:

> Ce qui m'a passionné c'est le paradoxe sur lequel l'oeuvre se
> clôt: Simon ne peut devenir chrétien et se prouver à lui-même
> qu'il l'est devenu qu'en épousant le destin des Juifs, "les plus

juifs de tous". Ceci revient à dire que le "nous autres" qui est en temps normal à la racine de tous les conformismes et des plus odieux pharisáismes, change de signe aussitôt qu'éclate la persécution. Il se déleste alors de tout faux sentiment de supériorité collective, de toute prétention. "On s'acharne contre toi; je suis là." C'est sur cet adsum que se clot *Le Signe de la croix.*[133]

Marcel closes his Postface to these two plays with the following poignant words, "Je songe avec une grande mélancolie qu'à trente-quatre ans d'intervalle ce *diptyque* dramatique fait en quelque manière pendant à mon *Seuil invisible.* Pourtant quel abîme sépare les deux livres, les deux dates! Combien de vies précieuses, combien de nobles espérances s'y sont engouffrées! ..."[134]

Dedicated to Jacques Hébertot, *Rome n'est plus dans Rome* was produced for the first time on April 19, 1951 at the Théâtre Hébertot.

The action of the play takes place in the winter of 1951. Pascal Laumière, the principal character, is a journalist. He has recently written a series of articles in a rightist weekly, which have classified him as enemy number one in the eyes of the Communists. His wife Renée has taken seriously an anonymous letter he received saying: "Les Communistes arrivent. Vous êtes sur la liste de ceux qui doivent être déportés. Prenez vos précautions."[135] Renée's half-sister, Esther, a widow devoted to her brother-in-law Pascal, tells Renée that she is sure that Pascal did not take this letter seriously. A cable arrives from a Carlos Martinez, a friend of Renée's who lives in Rio, offering Pascal a chair in French literature in a new university near Rio. Renée is determined that Pascal accept this position in order that the family may emigrate to a place of safety. When she tells Pascal about the offer, he answers that under no circumstances will he leave France. Renée then showers her husband with abuse, accusing him of not caring about her fate and the future of their two children, and adds

> Tu n'es pas quelqu'un de fort, Pascal, tu n'es pas sûr de toi. Et je te dirai autre chose que j'ai remarqué souvent: tu aimes accueillir,

même l'adversaire, surtout l'adversaire. C'est
parce que tu avais peur de toi, de ce que nos
amis appellent ton esprit d'hospitalité, que
tu n'as pas voulu rentrer à Paris sous
l'occupation alors que tu n'avais rien à
craindre sauf de toi-même ... C'est vraiment
la seule résistance dont tu puisses te vanter.
Mais peut-on appeler ça du courage? La
peur de la peur est-elle du courage?

Pascal,   (avec force.) Ecoute-moi. Il est par trop
facile de disqualifier tous nos actes, de les
imputer à l'égoisme ou la lâcheté ... mais je
ne sais rien de plus vil que ce plaisir de
discréditer, rien de plus aveuglant non plus.
Si j'avais peur d'avoir peur, comme tu dis, je
partirais.

Renée.   Tu partiras. Nous partirons.[136]

Esther has an only child, Marc-André, whose father was
killed in a concentration camp by the Germans. Pascal has
become a kind of adoptive father to the boy whom he dearly
loves. Marc-André has recently shown signs of instability.
Many of his friends have joined the Communist Party. While
he does not share their convictions and cannot go along with
them he does not want to be their victim.

Marc-André visits his uncle Pascal, who invites his confidence. Pascal tells the boy that it is his, Pascal's generation,
which is responsible for the present state of the world, "Nous
qui avons laissé dériver ce monde vers l'horreur et vers la
folie".[137] Marc-André answers that he does not understand
these things, that he is not much interested in history and
that the present suffices for him ... "il me suffirait si on
pouvait y respirer".[138]

Marc-André now tells Pascal that he has decided to leave
France with a friend whose father has a large business in
Equatorial Africa. He asks his uncle why he so severely
judges people who want to leave France saying that only
people who might be safe in remaining would be those who
are truly religious. He reminds his uncle that he, Marc-
André, has no religion; that he has met only one person
whom he considers truly religious; he is the father of a friend

Denis Moreuil who refused a position which was offered him in Mexico, telling his son

"Je ne sais pas ce que l'événement fera de moi, peut-être une loque, mais j'ai foi en Dieu, et je crois que le moment venu, je compte qu'il ne m'abandonnera pas, qu'il m'épargnera la suprême déchéance et qu'ou bien il me reprendra, ou bien il me donnera la force de supporter la torture."

Marc-André.   Ce sont là des paroles qui trouvent en moi un écho, bien qu'une telle foi me soit presque incompréhensible. Mais vous mon oncle, en toute conscience, est-ce que vous pourriez les prendre à votre compte?

Pascal,   (après un silence, humblement.) Non, en toute honnêteté je ne pourrais pas.[139]

It is after this conversation that Pascal decides to accept the position in South America and to take Esther and Marc-André together with his family.

The next scene finds the family in a small city San Felipe in Brazil. Renée and the children are quite content. Marc-André is happier than he has ever been. He is in love with Térèse, the niece of Carlos and he is waiting for a good post as tutor in a family. Only Pascal is depressed and is now being criticized for not going to Mass on Sundays. Though he is a Catholic he has never been in the habit of going to church. Also he is being criticized for taking walks in the evening with Esther.

One evening two weeks before Pascal's classes were to begin, a padre, Ricardo, from the near-by convent visits Pascal. The conversation falls on the liberal tendencies of some French Catholics.

Padre Ricardo.   Ce que vous nommez ouverture d'esprit pourrait bien être une brèche par laquelle beaucoup d'erreurs ont pénétré. Ici, dans ce pays d'outre-Atlantique, nous estimons que notre mission est de prémunir les intelligences contre ces erreurs qui ont été dénoncées tout récemment, et cet enseignement de la littérature pour lequel, sur la recommandation de personnes d'élite comme Carlos Martinez, vous avez été désigné, est précisément destiné dans notre pensé à tous à servir de bastion contre ces erreurs détestables qui ont mené L'Europe à sa perte.

Pascal, (sèchement.) Comme historien de la littérature, de la poésie, du roman, je vois assez mal en quoi je puis avoir à assurer cette défense.

Padre Ricardo. Vous me surprenez, cher monsieur. Dans une lutte ouverte entre l'Esprit-Saint et les puissances démoniaques qui se sont déchaînées dans le monde, il ne peut y avoir de neutralité en quelque domaine que ce soit, et surtout dans ce que vous appelez la littérature. Il ne s'agit pas seulement ou même principalement d'exposer, il faut juger, et juger selon les normes invariables ... Mais à la vérité, je suis sans inquiétude. Votre présence ici, parmi nous, prouve suffisamment que vous êtes avec nous dans ce grand combat.

Pascal. Avec vous?

Padre Ricardo. Je ne vous ferai pas l'injure de croire que votre départ vous a été dicte par des motifs purement personnels. Si vous avez quitté l'Europe, c'est que ce combat ne pouvait plus y être mené avec une chance quelconque de succès.

Pascal, (avec une ironie voilée.) Savez-vous, mon Père, que vous m'éclairez sur mes propres intentions?

Padre Ricardo. C'est ce lutteur tenace que nous avons accueilli parmi nous, seulement la bataille a ses règles auxquelles le soldat doit se soumettre. Et ces regles ne peuvent venir que de la plus haute autorité, c'est-à-dire de l'Eglise.

Pascal, (avec violence.) Mon Père, il y a entre nous un effroyable malentendu. Je n'ai pas choisi contre la liberté.

Padre Ricardo. Qu'appelez-vous la liberté?

Pascal.	Je n'ai pas choisi non plus contre la vérité ... et à mes yeux elles se confondent.[140]

As a result of this interview, Pascal decides to write a letter to the Rector of the University:

> La lettre que dans un instant j'écrirai au recteur de San Felipe créera une situation parfaitement nette. Ce refus de me plier à des exigences que ma conscience réprouve, c'est vraiment de Dieu véritable qui me l'a dicté ... et de ce jour je le reconnais, je m'engage envers lui, et il me semble que dans sa condescendance ou dans sa générosité ... car ce ne peut être un Dieu sans honneur.[141]

A few moments later Pascal addresses a radio message to France:

Pascal,	(d'une voix forte.) Mes amis de France, on m'a demande de m'addresser à vous une fois tous les quinze jours pour vous dire comment nous les émigrés, nous les transfuges, nous voyons la France ...
Marc-André.	Il a dit les transfuges! ...
Pascal.	... Il y a dans une tragédie de Corneille assez oubliée quelques vers fameux et d'ailleurs admirables. Sertorius, général rebelle en Espagne, proclame que c'est lui qui incarne la Rome véritable.
	Je n'appelle plus Rome un enclos de murailles;/Que ses proscriptions comblent de funerailles;/Ces murs, dont le destin fut autrefois si beau,/N'en sont que la prison, ou plutôt le tombeau:/ Mais pour revivre ailleurs dans sa première force;/Avec les faux Romains elle a fait plein divorce;/Et, comme autour de moi j'ai tous ses vrais appuis,/Rome n'est plus dans Rome, elle est toute ou je suis./ Mes amis, cette pensée est fausse; et c'est cela que je veux vous crier aujourd'hui. Nous avons eu tort de partir: il fallait rester, il fallait lutter sur place. L'illusion qu'on peut emporter sa patrie avec soi ne peut naître que de l'orgueil et de la plus folle présomption. Vous qui peut-être hésitez devant

> la menace de demain, restez, je vous en
> conjure, et si vous ne vous en sentez pas la
> force ... si vous n'en avez pas la force ...
>
> (il chancelle et s'abat sur le sol. Esther
> s'élance vers lui; à ce moment paraît un
> jeune moine d'expression ascétique et
> comme on veut lui barrier la route, il dit
> doucement.)

Le Moine. Madame, laissez-moi aller jusqu'à lui. Je sais
qu'il m'attend.[142]

This play which deals with a situation which could
possibly result from the Communist menace, is less convincing than the previous three plays which deal with the
historical fact of Nazi persecutions. Not that *Rome n'est plus
dans Rome's* premise lacks a reasonable basis, nor is it
essential to a good play that it have a reasonable basis.
Marcel, in a speech given in defense of the play states: "On
entrera dans cette pensée et dans cette oeuvre dans la mesure
précise où on aura su se détacher de toute préoccupation soit
politique, soit morale, comme peut le faire l'auditeur d'un
quatuor ou d'une symphonie. Le paradox, je le sais bien,
c'est qu'ici la matière même de la symphonie est faite de
sentiments, voire de passions relatives à une certaine
situation historique sans précédent. Mais mon ambition,
peut-être insensée, a été de montrer qu'avec tout cela on
peut malgré tout composer une musique."[143]

But the author has posed several important questions in
this play.

Should a person who does not know the extent of his
physical courage, or of his religious and spiritual strength,
seek to avoid a situation which would demand the test?
Marcel's protagonist, Pascal, finds that for him it was wrong
to flee, and so he tells the radio audience at the end of the
play "ne partez-pas—luttez sur place." The question arises
however as to whether Pascal would have discovered this
reservoir of spiritual strength without having left France. It
was only after he had experienced a threat to his liberty that
he was able to speak these words.

On the other hand the problem of Marc-André was solved
by leaving France. Removed from the atmosphere of the

preceding years in his own country, with its climate of
defeatism, and from his Communistic friends whose credo he
could not accept, he was able to establish himself happily in
the New World.

The second important question dealt with in *Rome n'est
plus dans Rome* concerns the attempt by an authoritarian
group to control education and freedom of thought. Pascal's
complete rejection of this attempt demonstrates his
intellectual and moral courage. In discussing this particular
problem in the aforementioned lecture, Marcel says:[144]

Nous vivons hélas! dans un monde de plus en plus coupé en
deux, et où un fanatisme suscite en face de lui un contre-
fanatisme. Les positions intermédiaires, c'est-à-dire au fond les
positions libérales au sens vrai et non caricatural de ce mot,
tendant de plus en plus à disparaître, et ceux qui veulent à tout
prix les maintenir étant condamnés à être pris dans cette sorte
d'étau. Pascal Laumière n'a été admis à enseigner à l'Université
de San Felipe au Brésil qu'à une condition: c'est de participer
activement à la lutte contre le communisme qu'il a refusé. Mais
prenons bien garde à ceci: du point de vue du cléricalisme
fanatique, ce n'est pas seulement le communisme qui est
condamné, c'est tout un ensemble d'idées dites subversives que,
par un décret absolument arbitraire de l'esprit, on assimile plus
ou moins directement au communisme. Nous ne savons que trop
ce qu'il y a de sommaire, et je dirai de totalitaire dans l'idée,
terriblement confuse, de contre-révolution. Lorsque Padre
Ricardo déclare qu'il n'y a pas de place pour la neutralité dans
la lutte sans merci entre l'Esprit-Saint et les puissances
démoniaques qui se sont déchaînées dans le monde, comment ne
pas voir qu'il entend confisquer ce qu'il appelle l'Esprit-Saint au
bénéfice d'une doctrine entendue d'ailleurs au sens le plus étroit,
le plus restrictif, et en fin de compte non point du tout de
l'Eglise entendue au seul sens véritable, c'est-à-dire universel,
mais de ceux qui indûment prétendent l'incarner ... Lorsque
Pascal dit qu'il est tombé dans un guet-apens, c'est l'exacte
vérité. Le Père prétend l'obliger à reconnaître qu'en acceptant la
chaire de San Felipe il a opté: sans quoi, dit-il, il faudrait
admettre que son départ n'a été qu'une fuite commandée par le
souci exclusif de sauvegarder sa sécurité personnelle. Telle est
l'espèce de chantage moral auquel se livre Padre Ricardo.
Chantage matériel aussi, car si Pascal ne se soumet pas, les

portes de l'université se fermeront devant lui, et comment pourra-t-il subsister?

The question of Faith and Grace as in previous plays assumes great importance. In this case Marcel links Faith and Grace to liberty. When he quotes the words of the father of Denis Moreuil who by reason of his faith believes he will be granted the Grace to withstand torture, Marcel is declaring that this man is now free. At the same time Marcel warns that true faith is something other than blind acceptance of a doctrine or adherence to a church whose practices may or may not be rooted in spiritual values: "J'ajouterai bien entendu que même des religions authentiques en leur principe resquent de dégénérer en idolâtrie là où la volonté de puissance vient les corrompre—et c'est hélas! ce qui tend à se produire chaque fois qu'une Eglise se trouve dotée de la puissance temporelle."[145]

As for characterization, Marcel created in Renée the most odious person in his theatre. She is completely different from Pauline, in *Le Signe de la croix*, whose understandable anxiety for the welfare of her family sometimes makes her unpleasant; Renée on the other hand is completely selfish and despicable in her attempts to undermine Pascal's confidence in himself. Pascal, who in the beginning seems another one of Marcel's weak men, takes on, as we get to know him better, a kind of tragic dignity. Marc-André is a completely plausible character. He had had no opportunity to know and to love the France to which Pascal gives his loyalty, and it is natural that he can adjust easily to a new environment.

Rome n'est plus dans Rome is the only play of Marcel's that I have ever seen on the stage. It comes to life vividly in a number of moving moments, but it must be said that its lengthy discussions sometimes spoil its dramatic effect and create the risk of its being classified as a play of ideas.

The themes of loneliness and lack of communication are expressed by every character.

Perhaps it must be admitted that *Rome n'est plus dans Rome* is above all a play of ideas which does not even have as its basis an actual situation, only a possible one. Since critics agree that nothing ages so quickly in the theatre as current problems, this play may lose all its significance in years to come. The characters, though well-drawn, are not examples of Marcel's best portrayals—Pascal and Esther particularly often lack real life. Marc-André is the most human and Renée in spite of her viciousness or perhaps because of it, creates a response. But in general the impression remains that in this play Marcel needed to get something off his chest, and in spite of some moving scenes, *Rome n'est plus dans Rome* does not rank among his best plays.

The following criticisms by Lalou, Lemarchand and Kemp grant Marcel his due as a good dramatist—but all express doubts about the value of this particular play. Mr. Lalou remarks:

> ... Grâce à la médiocrité de ce velléitaire, [Pascal] le dramaturge peut déployer autour de Laumière un eventail des réactions familiales devant ce projet d'exode et sa réalisation dans une Amérique ensoleillée. S'étonnera-t-on que le falot Pascal, aussi choqué par un rigide dominicain qu'il est séduit par un tendre franciscain nous touche moins que sa femme, la Renée, qui s'est vengée de se sentir son inférieure en l'avilissant peu à peu.
>
> ... Tandis que Pascal pérore devant sa belle soeur ou devant le micro, c'est cette complicité entre Renée Laumière, et G. M. qui nous fait reconnaître en ce philosophe un véritable auteur dramatique.[146]

Mr. Lemarchand praises the play thus:

> ... Mais elle doit plaire pour des vertues plus proprement dramatiques, et auxquelles je suis infiniment plus sensible qu'à celles que j'ai dites. Il ya a, dans les trois premiers actes, une vivacité, une justesse de ton, une nécessité dramatique qui font qu'il n'y a pas un temps mort ... La description de l'effon-drement de la résistance de Pascal a tous les mérites d'une action vive et surprenante, en même temps qu'elle marche d'un pas égal vers la conclusion ...[147]

And in *Théâtre de France*, Mr. Kemp writes:

> La clarté, la vigueur des trois premiers actes nous ont conquis. Il me faut avouer que les deux autres nous laissent hésitants et à demi désemparés. Le problème religieux se substitue à

l'improviste aux problèmes moins universels, mais, dans l'actualité, plus neufs et très pressants de la fidélité à la patrie, de la confiance qu'on lui doit garder. La foi, et spécialement la foi catholique joue le personnage *ex machina* qui, sans les résoudre, "evanouit" les difficultés qu'on nous exposait ai chaudement. Nous ne comprenons plus "Mais les trois premiers actes, j'ai joie à le redire, sont dans leur sévérité constamment captivants, angoissants. Je me demande même s'ils ne sont pas dangereux. C'est un attrait de plus; et une inquiétude, de surcroît.[148]

* * *

After Hitler's war it was inevitable, because of Marcel's background and innate sensitivity, that he should become involved in the problems with which his four plays deal during this period. The plays concern both Hitlerism and Communism, but it is the effect of these ideologies rather than a discussion of principles, which keeps these from being thesis plays. Character portrayal, psychological soundness and interesting plots make them dramatically good. Even the most abstract one, *Rome n'est plus dans Rome*, is good drama when seen on the stage, whether in 1950 or during its revival in 1952.

One comment should be added here. In these plays there is undeniable identification of the author with his characters. Marcel is not only observing and analyzing the people he has created. He is these charactrers not any one of them, but something of each of them.

He is Pascal Laumière, journalist and professor in *Rome n'est plus dans Rome*, who believes in the Communist domination of France, who doubts his own strength to withstand torture, and who later in the new world rebels against the tyranny of dictation which would destroy his academic freedom. He is a man of the Résistance in *L'Emissaire*, and at the same time he is a man unable to do heroic or violent acts. In *Le Signe de la croix* he is Simon the Jew who has no religious affiliation and he is tante Léna the pious Jewess. He is also the benevolent Abbé Schweigsam.

Marcel the dramatist expressed objectively through his

characters all points of view; Marcel the man could not hold himself aloof during this tragic period of emotional stress.

5—Social Conflicts

Mon Temps n'est pas le vôtre
Croissez et multipliez

The last two plays, both published in 1955, are Marcel's most recent dramatic works that I consider. Regarded super-ficially, they might be classified as thesis plays and con-sidered reversions to his first works. This would be a false estimate. Though the plays grapple with ideas, the author does not attempt to preach, and the characters are not puppets. The subjects handled are, in the first, conflicting concepts of art; and in the second, the practice of religion.

In presenting certain social mores and their effect on the individual and society, Marcel does not attempt any easy solutions. His characters suffer from loneliness and lack of communication as do those in previous plays; but the problems are not personal only.

As the theme for *Mon Temps n'est pas le vôtre*, Marcel chose the tendency of youth to embrace everything new simply because it is new and its willingness to discard a heritage and to replace the beautiful and true by the smart and the bold.

Marcel is far from being a conservative. He loves young people. He is very much interested in and receptive to new ideas but he has a genuine fear for the future of a world where the younger generation is ready to discard as out-moded all the old values, and eager to glorify new painting, new music, new literature, without the ability to assess their merits. Some of the situations in the following play may seem exxaggerated but they describe a group of this insecure youth who wish to be chic at any cost. The play is also an indictment of those of the older generation who lack the courage to oppose these ideas.

Alfred Champel, married to a garrulous and unintelligent

woman, is the father of two daughters, Marie Henriette and
Perrine. These two are the younger generation in its most
unattractive sense. The father is completely disgusted with
the point of view and habits of his daughters; the mother, on
the other hand, always takes their part. The girls have just
returned from a cruise to Greece and Asia Minor; the
parents were forced to forego a vacation because of the
expense of their cruise.

Champel.	Elles ont déclaré que l'Acropole les avait déçues. Les temples leur ont paru trop blancs.
Madame Champel.	Pas assez blancs, Alfred.
Champel.	Pas à leur idée, en tout cas.
Madame Champel.	Elles ont des goûts personnels; on ne peut pas le leur reprocher.
Champel,	(caustique.) Du reste, il paraît que tout ce bateau a été déçu par le Parthénon. Le bateau suivant a été admiratif. C'est à n'y rien comprendre ...[149]

It is quite evident that the household is not a happy one.
Champel is also not happy in his professional life. He is the
director of a Ministry and has nothing to look forward to but
his retirement. The result is his almost constant bad humor.
The fact that he has no son is also a source of great
unhappiness to him.

One day Flavio Romanelli, a young Italian pianist and
composer comes to call on Champel. Champel had known
Flavio's mother when he spent some time in Italy as a youth.
The young man has come to Paris to prepare for "le prix
North Blessington" which carries with it much money and
wide publicity. Flavio tells Champel that although he would
like to have the prize he is not nearly so eager for it as is his
fiancée, Diane, who thinks that publicity will give him a
chance to concertize and make money to pay for a house.
Then they can marry and have children. Flavio's chief
interest is in music composition but Diane knows there is
little money in this and discourages him.

Meanwhile Flavio has sent one of his compositions to a
great musician and conductor, Emile Keyser. Keyser accepts

Flavio's new concerto and plans to have his orchestra play it with Flavio as piano soloist. When the program is announced there is an uproar among the *avant-garde* led by some young musicians jealous because Keyser has refused to play their works.

Flavio.

Keyser ne redoute pas cette cabale pour lui-même; il la méprise, il est courageux, il déteste cette vilénie. Mais il pense que ce tumulte risque de me faire du tort pour le prix North Blessington. Il me conseille de réfléchir.[150]

It is decided that the concerto will not be played. Champel, who is dismayed about the whole occurrence says to his daughters:

Bien sûr, bien sûr, mon temps n'est pas le vôtre. Mais c'est que votre temps n'est plus celui des hommes réels, c'est celui des robots, pis encore, c'est le temps illusoire que projettent devant eux des cerveaux affolés par le désir de dissembler ...

Parbleu! Si tu t'en doutais, ce ne serait pas vrai. Comme toute votre génération, comme les artistes et les écrivains que vous admirez, vous êtes des conformistes à rebours; vous vous évertuez à prendre le contrepied de ce qu'on a toujours pensé, toujours cru. Votre audace prétendue est la pire des lâchetés. Dans ce monde où chacun entend se signulariser, le seul courage qui vaille est de refuser cette fausse originalité devant laquelle les imbéciles plient les genoux parce qu'ils ont peur de passer pour rétrogrades. Ce qui est si admirable chez ce petit Flavio, c'est qu'il n'y a pas trace chez lui de cette prétention, de cette lâcheté.[151]

Goaded beyond control by the activities of his daughters and their friends, one day Champel makes the statement that he has every reason to believe that Flavio is his son. This assertion is false and Champel's brief association with Flavio's mother had been completely platonic. The impulse to make this statement was caused by his attraction to the serious, fervently artistic boy, whose ideals were so opposite to those of his own children and whom he longed to have had as a son.

Shortly thereafter Champel who had been suffering from a cardiac ailment suddenly dies, just before Flavio brings his mother from Italy to see her old friend.

Flavio marries his materialistic little fiancée, saying to Marie Henriette, who meanwhile has fallen in love with him:

> Dans quelques jours je serai l'époux de Diana. C'est aupres d'elle que je mènerai, je le sais maintenant, une vie pesante et misérable. Je crois encore que le don céleste m'avait été accorde, mais je sais maintenant qu'il m'a été retiré.[152]

This ends the rather slim plot which Marcel uses to advance an interesting idea. The play cannot be seriously considered as a good dramatic work; there are, however, some observations to be made. Marcel himself says, "La différence de climat entre *Mon Temps n'est pas le vôtre*, et la plupart de mes pièces est sans doute de nature à déconcerter le lecteur. Pour moi-même, elle constitue jusqu'à un certain point un sujet d'étonnement."[153]

It is an astonishing play for the student of Marcel's work as well as for its author. There is practically no characteristic of Marcel's previous work to be found in it.

Ainsi, plus peut-être qu'aucun autre de mes ouvrages, celui-ci se présente à moi comme une certaine aventure qui m'est intelligible a posteriori à la façon d'une histoire qu'on m'aurait racontée. Ce n'est sûrement pas un hasard si j'ai écrit cette pièce à un monent où ma répugnance pour le *tout fait*, pour le *préfabriqué* passe toute mesure. Certes, il me paraîtrait absurde de m'attacher à déconcerter des lecteurs, voire des commentateurs qui se seraient établis dans une certaine interprétation de mon oeuvre. Ce ne pourrait être là qu'un jeu dépourvu de toute signification authentique. Mais je crois discerner comme l'exaucement d'un voeu profond de mon être dans une pièce comme celle-ci, où le comique et le tragique sont plus intimement liés qu'en aucun autre de mes écrits. Ceci encore vaut d'être souligné.[154]

I was among those who were invited to the Galerie Daveche to hear a reading of this play by actors from the Comédie Française. The audience was convulsed with laughter by the humorous parts which referred to the girls' opinions on the art treasures of Greece. This opening scene immediately set the tone for something different in the way of a play by Gabriel Marcel.

After the reading, there was a discussion period in which André Maurois was the chairman, Robert Kemp the anti-critic, with Marcel defending his play. Everyone showed a spirit of good-will and Marcel maintained an objective attitude toward his play which at one point became extremely amusing. When Kemp asked him why he had killed off Champel, Marcel answered, "I have no idea. No one could have been more surprised that I when he died!"

Marcel denies that this is a *pièce à thèse*. When asked to what degree he is in agreement with Champel and Flavio on the subject of modern art and music, he answered that his personal position was of no importance. But the following words written in the Postface to the play, do express Marcel's attitude:

Mais, pensai-je, la nouveauté n'est pas en elle-même une valeur, elle ne doit jamais être recherchée pour soi. Les plus grands parmi les artistes ont bien rarement voulu être des novateurs. S'ils ont innové, c'est en général parce qu'ils y étaient intérieurement poussés, et peut-être le plus souvent ne fut-ce pas sans angoisse, car ils avaient pour la plupart le plus grand respect pour une tradition à laquelle ils se voyaient cependant tenus de porter atteinte. Quelle différence avec les artistes d'aujourd'hui qui ne respectant et ne reconnaissent plus aucune valeurs en dehors de celles qu'ils ont l'ambition d'instaurer, qui d'ailleurs, bien souvent, ne paraissent pas avoir une nature qui leur soit propre, et spéculent je ne dis pas seulement sur le snobisme, mais sur la peur qu'ont tant de gens "au courant" de paraître dépassés ou de l'être en effet; car chez eux l'être n'est plus que paraître.[155]

The final play, *Croissez et Multipliez*, which like the preceding one has a sociological theme, comes closer to being a thesis play than any written by Marcel since 1914. Marcel presented me with the proof sheets of this play just before I left Paris in August 1955, saying, "I know you will need this to bring me up to date." Two weeks before this he had invited me to hear a reading of the play, this time in a private home and again read by members of the Comédie Française. About fifty people were present among whom were important critics who received the reading with enthusiasm, though doubt was expressed as to whether it would be acceptable to the theatre-going public. Marcel himself says: "Plus sans doute qu'aucune autre de mes pièces, celle-ci est une pièce à problème, je ne dis pas une pièce à thèse, la distinction est essentielle et j'y reviendrai. Bien que je me rappelle à vrai dire assez mal les conditions dans lesquelles cet ouvrage a germé, en moi, je puis affirmer que je ne suis pas parti du problème pris par lui-même; c'est plutôt après avoir écrit la pièce que j'ai été amené au cours de conversations particulières, à constater son ampleur sur le plan social."[156]

The story is about Agnès, wife of Thierry Courteuil. Agnès is the daughter of a minor diplomat. She has lived most of her life in the secondary posts that her father had successively occupied and when Thierry, who for a long time had been captive in Germany, comes back home and they meet, Agnès is attracted to him. The goodness of his character is apparent and despite his experience he appears to be "un homme neuf, intact".[157] The fact that he is a believer seems in the beginning to have been an attraction to Agnès—a relief from the political conservatism and religious scepticism of her life with her parents. When the play begins, Agnès is pregnant with her sixth child. She has borne a child each year since her marriage and now she is in a state bordering on hysteria. She sees ahead the incessant malaises which have preceded each birth and is rebellious and completely disillusioned with marriage and all that pertains to it. Thierry, a born family man, while deploring the fact that Agnès experiences difficult months with each pregnancy, is perfectly content with the state of affairs. he is scrupulously conforming to the prescriptions of the church, he loves his children, his conscience is clear and he has the complete approval of l'Abbé Petit-Paul, his close friend and spiritual advisor who shared his captivity during the war. Their friendship is a source of mounting irritation to Agnès. Agnés is a passionate musician and resents the fact that her domestic responsibilities make it practically impossible for her to spend any time at the piano.

Agnès. C'est tout de même littéralement vrai, tu sais, que trois mesures peuvent nous transporter dans un autre monde où il n'y a plus ni ennuis domestiques, ni servitude conjugale, plus de disputes, de comptes à régler et de végétations à enlever ... Pourtant ce monde-là ce n'est pas la mort, c'est la perfection.[158]

Agnès feels herself exiled from "la vraie vie". Marcel quotes the famous phrase of Rimbaud and tells us that at first he had intended to give this play the title "La Vrai Vie est absente".

In spite of her resentment and present unhappiness Agnès is really not unfair in her judgments concerning her husband. She sees that he is not selfish, but she cannot help being exasperated by him.

Agnès. Thierry n'est pas un homme-femme, c'est un homme-maman,—un homme-nounou. Il est patient, expert, vigilant. Il adore langer les petits, les mettre sur le pot, les torcher. Au début je trouvais ca attendrissant, maintenant ça m'exaspère.[159]

Agnès is by no means a superficial person and, beyond these irritations, she begins to question the significance of her life and the value of life in general, "cette 'chose' indéfinissable dont la transmission s'effectue selon un mécanisme propre à éveiller la répugnance et même la dérision, cette 'chose' a-t-elle vraiment un sens". "La vie qui bourgeonne en nous obstinément, stupidement, ignoblement, la vie qui fabrique une tumeur comme elle fabrique un petit enfant, avec la même application, la même tenacité imbécile ... Je déteste la vie."[160]

These words recall a passage from Marcel's play written thirty years previously, *Un Homme de Dieu* where Osmonde under completely different circumstances says in substance the same thing. "... recevoir quoi? donner quoi? Et puis justement si c'est pour transmettre à d'autres qui transmettront à leur tour, à quoi bon ce jeu, cette course perpétuelle dans le brouillard."[161]

Agnès becomes more and more exasperated with the Abbé Petit-Paul and his intrusions in the life of her family. She finally refuses to receive him in the home, telling Thierry, "Il nous traite tous comme des scouts."

Beside the Abbé there is another character of major importance in the play. He is Bruno, Agnès' cousin. Some years previously, he had suddenly taken Dominican orders, greatly to the surprise of his family and friends. now, on his first visit home, Agnès sees in him the personification of purity, for he had chosen "la rupture délibérée avec le jeu accablant et grotesque de la procréation".[162] She tells Bruno's sister, Chantal Forge, who is her greatest friend, that she considers Bruno a saint and that she will beg him to help her. In her first attempt to confess to Bruno, he repulses her summarily, but later he seeks her and tells her, "Agnès, sans doute n'y a-t-il rien de plus impur au monde que cette hantise de la pureté, cette obsession qui vous habite."[163]

Bruno then tells Agnès that he is leaving France and will probably never return. He had joined the Dominicans after his sister Chantal announced her intention to marry Guillaume Forge, who was his friend. The intolerable jealousy which her announcement awakened in him brought him the realization of the nature of his friendship for Guillaume.

Agnès.	Mais alors, vous voulez dire? ...
Bruno.	Oui. Ce que j'avais pris pour de l'amitié méritait un tout autre nom. J'eus ainsi la révélation que j'étais voué à ces amours condamnées. Si je n'avais pas été croyant, je pense que je me serais suicidé, ou bien, peut-être aurais-je accepté, subi ... J'ai choisi l'autre voie.
Agnès.	Mais êtes-vous certain que ce n'était pas un autre suicide?
Bruno.	Il m'est arrivé de me le demander, mais ce n'est pas vrai.[164]

Chantal's husband, Guillaume Forge, deserts her and goes to live with Corinne, Agnès' sister, with whom he has been having an affair. Chantal accepts Agnès' invitation to live with her family, and through helping to care for Agnès' children Chantal is happier than she has ever been before. She and Thierry are compatible and these facts cause Agnès to decide she can now leave her family. She tells Thierry "je voudrais trouver dans quelque milieu misérable une tâche à remplir."[165] She realizes that her real task lies at home with her family but says "elle me répugne, ou bien, peut-être n'en suis-je plus digne."[166]

In the final scene Thierry tells Agnès that the Abbé Petit-Paul is coming to speak with her. At first Agnès refuses to receive him, then consents, saying that this will be their final meeting.

Agnès,	(se contenant difficilement.) Monsieur l'Abbé, j'aurais voulu que cet entretien me fût épargné, mais si vraiment il le faut …
	… votre direction, 'jaimerais mieux dire votre intrusion, nous a déjà fait le plus grand mal à Thierry et à moi, tellement de mal que le pire est arrivé, du moins ce qui de votre point de vue est le pire, puisque je vais très vraisemblablement partir …
	… Si j'avais la lâcheté de rester, je ferais souffrir les autres. Non, je n'infligerai pas mon amertume à mes enfants, ni même à Thierry qui est un enfant, lui aussi. Sans doute irrémédiablement, oui, pour toujours un enfant. Ma cousine occupera ma place, au moins quelque temps, sa vie est détruite, j'avais craint à tort, oui, bien à tort, que sa raison ne chavirât, mais elle a une âme qui peut encore fleurir. La mienne, non. Mais je ne suis pas encore prête à accepter ce desséchement ou cette corruption. Et votre responsabilité dans tout cela est trop lourde pour que je vous accorde le droit de me condamner.
L'Abbé,	(avec une grande douceur.) Je ne vous condamne pas, Agnès, de nous trois je suis tenté

de penser qu'en effet le vrai coupable c'est moi.[167]

The Abbé continues "c'est ce mea culpa que je suis venu articuler devant vous." He convinces Agnès that she must not leave her family and she consents to try again. The three principal characters speak as follows at the conclusion of the play:

Agnès.	Moi je crois que je commence seulement à me mettre en route et je ne sais si je ne fléchirai pas dès la première étape.
Thierry.	J'avais voulu fonder un foyer chrétien, mais qu'est-ce qu'un foyer sans la flamme? et la flamme c'est la joie. Mon contentement n'était pas la joie, il est devenu ta souffrance et ton amertume ...
L'Abbé,	(profondément.) Il n'y a pas de solution, chacun doit prier pour trouver sa voie, et je crois—mais cela, je le dis en tremblant—que le Souverain Pontife et ceux qui l'assistent, doivent prier, eux aussi. Il ne leur est pas permis non plus de s'établir dans des formules. Imaginer, réfléchir prier, nul n'en est dispensé.[168]

It is easy to see that if this play is widely read, and should it ever be produced in France, there will be serious repercussions. Though Marcel says "ce problème est posé aux consciences par l'attitude rigide qu'adopte l'Eglise catholique en ce qui concerne les relations conjugales regardées par elle comme ordonnées à une fin unique: la procréation",[169] he is really attacking not only the Church's interdiction of birth control, but he is challenging its entire intrusion into the daily life of its adherents and its interference with the structure of our civilization. He warns that such repressive injunctions can lead to heresy. He expresses this idea categorically in the following exchange between Agnès and the Abbé:

Agnès	Mais enfin, quelles qu'aient été vos erreurs ou vos ... pardonnez-moi, vos maladresses, vous n'avez formulé que des préceptes que

L'Abbé.

Agnès.

n'importe quel prêtre catholique aurait pris à son compte. Si Thierry changeait de directeur, le problème resterait le même ... Vous devez comprendre qu'il est insoluble ...

Moi, voyez-vous, ce sont ces préceptes contre lesquels je m'insurge. Je n'ai jamais été une catholique bien fervente, mais ils auront fait de moi une hérétique. Et c'est encore une raison pour que je m'en aille. Après tout, Thierry a bien le droit de vouloir que ses enfants partagent sa foi, et cette foi, je suis assez contradictoire pour l'admirer, même si elle me révolte.[170]

Marcel says that Faith is something other than precepts to be obeyed blindly. "Qui sait si nous n'obéissons pas à des consignes inventées il y a des millénaires, au non de principes auxquelles nous ne croyons plus."[171]

The play presents rather complete evidence of Marcel's anti-clerical position. He is attacking practices, not men. However foolish and short-sighted are the Petit-Pauls in the service of the Church, they must not bear the blame. They only perform their duties. The Abbé discovers that "il n'a pas su comprendre *du dedans* des difficultés qu'il était trop enclin à résoudre *du dehors* et que d'ailleurs son intrusion a fait beaucoup plus de mal que de bien".[172]

And finally Petit-Paul makes an observation which may lie at the heart of the whole question of the relationship of the Church to daily life.

Au fond, ce que l'Eglise exige, ici comme ailleurs, c'est l'héroisme. Mais, dans la vie quotidienne, personne n'est disposé à se comporter en héros. C'est une vague possibilité qu'on réserve pour les grandes occasions: la guerre, la persécution ... Alors, au jour le jour, on installe chez soi le mensonge et l'hypocrisie.

Bien sûr, l'Eglise est au-dessus de ces misères là. Mais l'Eglise, ici, qui est-ce? Oh! je sais bien, je connais la réponse des manuels. Il faudrait se contenter de lire les écriteaux, et il y a des moments où on me peut plus ...[173]

Because of the importance of the ideas dealt with in the

play, one might imagine that dramatic interest would be completely secondary. This is absolutely not true. In the competent hands of the actors who read it, the play became extremely exciting theatre. The main characters are magnificently developed. Agnès is classical in her fury. Thierry, basically another Marcel man, weak, but this time appealing; the Abbé entirely plausible. The introduction of Bruno and his problem seems at first unnecessary as it introduces the discussion of a completely different problem; it was undoubtedly done to demonstrate to Agnès that the man who represented her ideal of purity was less pure than her husband. The Bruno situation is similar to that in Martin du Gard's *Un Taciturne* produced 28 October, 1931.

It is interesting here to note the extreme popularity of such plays as *Les Dialogues des Carmélites* and *Port Royal* in France. These plays include long discussions of subjects that would at first appear to have little interest for the average theatre-goer. *Croissez et multipliez* could be rejected on the basis of the very long discussions but prejudice is much more likely to prevent the production of this play which deals with a highly controversial but important contemporary theme. Marcel voiced a doubt as to whether this play would have interest for a reader or spectator who is not Catholic, but he feels that it is significant that "au milieu de l'effroyable désarroi contemporain et comme en réaction contre un avilissement sans nom de toute une partie de la littérature,, une mystérieuse polarisation des consciences tend à s'effectuer autour des affirmations les plus hautes qui aient jamais été proferées, celles dont le sujet et j'oserai dire le lieu ne se situent pas sur la terre".[174]

* * *

To be judged as permanently vital, a play must deal with matters essential to life, not only with those of an epoch. The post World War II plays of Gabriel Marcel—*Le Dard,* *L'Emissaire, Le Signe de la croix* and *Rome n'est plus dans Rome*, though they faithfully and even passionately depict and reflect life, pose problems of a particular period, under circumstances which could only have existed at that particular time.

The subjects handled in Marcel's two latest plays are not limited to a particular time or circumstance. In *Le Coeur des autres* and in *Le Quatuor en Fa dièze* art plays an important role; but in these plays the subject is viewed in relation to its effect on individual or family relationships. In *Mon temps n'est pas le vôtre*, Marcel concerns himself with the changing concepts of art which affect universal standards.

In *Croissez et multipliez* the situation is the same. Discussion of religion in previous plays is subjective: What is the effect of religion or the lack of it on a personality or a family? In the latest plays the horizon widens and the emphasis is upon practices of religion and their universal application.

In the course of Marcel's career as a dramatist from 1914 to the present, he has covered a great span of ideas, beginning with rather abstract, ideological conflicts, through the effects upon individuals and communities after two world wars, to subjects of general importance. It is a broad canvas; a mirror reflecting a long period which many of us will recognize.

NOTES

[1] *L'Existentialisme chrétien*, p. 270.
[2] P. 56.
[3] P. 79.
[4] P. 143.
[5] P. 263.
[6] P. 387.
[7] *Existentialisme chrétien*, Regard en arrière, p. 312.
[8] P. 313.
[9] *Les Nouvelles Littéraires*, January 16, 1957.
[10] *L'Horizon*, postface, p. 179.
[11] *Ibid.*, pp. 179 f.
[12] *Ibid.*, p. 180.
[13] *Ibid.*, pp. 189 f.
[14] *Ibid.*, p. 189.
[15] *La Chapelle ardente*, p. 34.
[16] *Ibid.*, p. 61.
[17] *Ibid.*, p. 181.
[18] Postface.
[19] *La Chapelle ardente*, p. 164.
[20] Postface.

21 Postface.

22 J. J. Gautier, *Théâtre de France*, p. 6.

23 R. Lalou, "Une Homme de Dieu", *Théâtre de France*.

24 *Le mort de demain*, p. 139.

25 *L'Horizon*, postface, p. 181.

26 *Le Mort de demain*, p. 147.

27 *Ibid.*, p. 118.

28 *Rome n'est plus dans Rome*, p. 49.

29 *Le Mort de demain*, p. 161.

30 *Le Regard neuf*, p. 12.

31 *Ibid.*, p. 46.

32 *Ibid.*, p. 101.

33 *Ibid.*, p. 98.

34 *Ibid.*, p. 24.

35 *Ibid.*, p. 102.

36 *Le Monde cassé*, p. 70.

37 *Ibid.*, p. 71.

38 *Ibid.*, p. 70.

39 *Ibid.*, p. 71.

40 *Ibid.*

41 *Ibid.*, p. 51.

42 E. Jaloux, *Les Nouvelles littéraires*, January 16, 1957.

43 *Ibid.*

44 Jean-Jacques Bernard, *Le Feu qui reprend mal*, 1921; Paul Raynal, *Le Tombeau sous l'Arc de Triomphe*, 1924; Marcel Pagnol and Paul Nivoix, *Les Marchands de gloire*, 1925; Jean Giraudoux, *Siegfried*, 1928; and many others. The inclusion of Giraudoux's *Siegfried* may be questionable because Giraudoux has created Siegfried as a *symbol* as well as a war-hero.

46 *Un Homme de Dieu*, p. 194.

47 *Le Coeur des autres*, p. 73.

48 *Ibid.*, p. 102.

49 *Ibid.*, p. 116.

50 *Ibid.*, p. 118.

51 *Ibid.*, p. 132.

52 *Ibid.*, p. 49.

53 *Ibid.*, p. 29.

54 *Ibid.*, p. 112.

55 *Le Quatuor en fa dièse*, p. 191.

56 G. Marcel, "Regard en arrière", *L'Existentialisme chrétien*, p. 297.

57 *Le Quatuor en fa dièse*, pp. 26 f.

58 *Ibid.*, p. 30.

59 *Ibid.*, p. 34.

60 *Ibid.*, pp. 34 f.

61 *Ibid.*, pp. 178 f.

62 *Ibid.*, p. 189.

63 *Journal métaphysique*, p. 29.

64 *Ibid.*

65 *Ibid.*

66 *Ibid.*

67 R. Troisfontaines, *La Notion de présence chez Gabriel Marcel*, p. 203.

68 Mortier, *Quinze ans de théâtre, 1917-1932*, p. 165.

69 *Un Homme de Dieu*, p. 61.

70 *Ibid.*, pp. 189-192.

[71] *Rome n'est plus dans Rome*, pp. 42 f.
[72] R. Lalou, "Un Homme de Dieu", *Théâtre de France*, 1951.
[73] Y. Gandon, "Un Homme de Dieu", *Illustration*, June 11, 1949.
[74] *Le Chemin de Crête*, pp. 49 f.
[75] *Ibid.*, pp. 54 f.
[76] *Ibid.*, p. 72.
[77] *Ibid.*, p. 126.
[78] *Ibid.*, pp. 188 f.
[79] *Ibid.*, pp. 198 f.
[80] *Ibid.*, p. 246.
[81] *Le Revue théâtrale*, October–November, 1946.
[82] *Le Chemin de Crête*, p. 224.
[83] E. Jaloux, *Les Nouvelles littéraires*, January 16, 1937.
[84] M. A. Bellesort, *Le Plaisir du théâtre*.
[85] *Le Fanal*, p. 12.
[86] *Ibid.*, p. 37.
[87] *Ibid.*, pp. 55 f.
[88] *Ibid.*, p. 61.
[89] *Ibid.*, p. 48.
[90] *Ibid.*, p. 40.
[91] M. Martin du Gard, "Review of *Le Fanal*", *Les Nouvelles littéraires*, April 30, 1938.
[92] H. Bidou, "Review of *Le Fanal*", *Marianne*, May 4, 1938.
[93] E. Jaloux, *Les Nouvelles littéraires*, January 16, 1937.
[94] *La Table Ronde*, 1952.
[95] *Les Coeurs avides*, p. 61.
[96] *Ibid.*, pp. 74 f.
[97] *Ibid.*, p. 113.
[98] *Ibid.*, p. 157.
[99] *Ibid.*, p. 146.
[100] *Ibid.*, p. 146.
[101] *Ibid.*, p. 158.
[102] *Le Dard*, p. 51.
[103] *Ibid.*, p. 111.
[104] *Ibid.*, p. 117.
[105] *Ibid.*, p. 115.
[106] *Ibid.*, p. 118.
[107] *Ibid.*, p. 59.
[108] *Ibid.*, p. 57.
[109] *Ibid.*, p. 118.
[110] E. Jaloux, *Les Nouvelles littéraires*, January 16, 1937.
[111] *Vers un autre royaume*, postface, p. 231.
[112] *L'Emissaire*, p. 59.
[113] *Ibid.*, p. 79.
[114] *Vers un autre royaume*, postface, p. 233.
[115] "L'Emissaire," *Vers un autre royaume*, p. 104.
[116] Postface, *op. cit.*, p. 234.
[117] "L'Emissaire", *op. cit.*, p. 108.
[118] G. Marcel, Review of "Les Nuits de la colère", *La Revue théâtrale*, February 1947.
[119] *Ibid.*
[120] Postface, *Vers un autre royaume*, p. 233.
[121] *Ibid.*, p. 231.

122 "Le Signe de la croix", *op. cit.*, p. 139.
123 *Ibid.*, p. 161.
124 *Ibid.*, pp. 171 ff.
125 *Ibid.*, p. 204.
126 *Ibid.*, p. 207.
127 *Ibid.*, p. 220.
128 *Ibid.*, pp. 222 f.
129 *Ibid.*, p. 224.
130 *Ibid.*, p. 228.
131 *Ibid.*, p. 225.
132 *Ibid.*, p. 232.
133 Postface, *op. cit.*, p. 232.
134 *Ibid.*, p. 236.
135 *Rome n'est plus dans Rome*, p. 11.
136 *Ibid.*, pp. 64 f.
137 *Ibid.*, p. 40.
138 *Ibid.*
139 *Ibid.*, pp. 49 f.
140 *Ibid.*, pp. 116 ff.
141 *Ibid.*, p. 146.
142 *Ibid.*, pp. 147 f.
143 Extrait d'une conférence donnée au Théâtre Hébertot, le 15 mai, 1951.
144 *Ibid.*, p. 162.
145 Postface, p. 172.
146 R. Lalou, *Les Nouvelles Littéraires*, January 1951.
147 J. Lemarchand, *Le Figaro littéraire*, April 21, 1951.
148 R. Kemp, *Théâtre de France*, 1951.
149 *Mon Temps n'est pas le vôtre*, p. 2.
150 *Ibid.*, p. 205.
151 *Ibid.*, p. 185.
152 *Ibid.*, p. 235.
153 Postface, *op.cit.*, p. 237.
154 *Ibid.*, p. 245.
155 *Ibid.*, p. 238.
156 Postface, *Croissez et multipliez*, p. 201.
157 *Ibid.*, p. 202.
158 *Croissez et multipliez*, p. 20.
159 *Ibid.*, p. 11.
160 *Ibid.*
161 *Un Homme de Dieu*, Act 2, Scene 1.
162 *Croissez et multipliez*, p. 69.
163 *Ibid.*, p. 94.
164 *Ibid.*, p. 172.
165 *Ibid.*, p. 173.
166 *Ibid.*
167 *Ibid.*, p. 182.
168 *Ibid.*, pp. 198 f.
169 Postface, *loc.cit.*, p. 211.
170 *Croissez et multipliez*, p. 187.
171 *Ibid.*, p. 254.
172 *Ibid.*, p. 186.
173 *Ibid.*, p. 189.
174 Postface, *op.cit.*, p. 213.

Part Three

CHAPTER IV

The Place of Gabriel Marcel in Twentieth-Century Drama

At the turn of the century it was impossible to foresee clearly the future trend of the drama. It was evident that Naturalism was finished. It had been a school more interested in theory than in art, and therefore it was doomed in spite of the brilliance and the satire of a Becque. Many directions were indicated, various groups were striving to fulfill their own genius, innovating or imitating. Some were striving to explore the confines of science in abnormal phenomena or abnormalities of the personality. Others were experimenting with psychological phenomena or mysticism or religious ecstacy.

The important thing was that for a quarter of a century French literature had received more than it had given. It had been a period when foreign literature of every genre had poured into France and had exerted influence on French thinking. In the field of drama it was Ibsen who was the important influence. Ibsen brought back to the French theatre the importance of ideas. In his drama he showed the struggle of personalities and the problem of the individual striving to express himself in accordance with his innate endowment in the face of exterior forces created by society. This theatre was continued in France by Curel, Hervieu and others and it was in this tradition that Marcel started to write his plays.

It is evident that Marcel was greatly influenced by Ibsen. The so-called problem play or play of ideas with intensely real characters called for qualities of observation and under-standing of human personality. What science is now attempting to accomplish in the realm of psycho-analysis and psychology, Ibsen knew intuitively. He realized the

151

supreme importance of the individual, and he felt the tragedy caused by denial of love between individuals and between the individual and society. Added to this was his passion for ideas as expressed in *A Doll's House, Ghosts, An Enemy of the People.* He never caused his protagonists to be mere mouthpieces to express these ideas. The characters became the ideas in flesh, and it is difficult to find in these plays a single speech that is out of character. This was a new European theatre in the middle of the nineteenth century.

It is possible that the young Gabriel Marcel was attracted not only by the work of Ibsen but by his life. Ibsen, the embodiment of the lonely man, must have appealed to this young writer whose plays were already stressing the tragedy of loneliness in the world.

Ibsen's belief that the final wrongs and the greatest tragedies in human life stem from the denial of love, is shared by Marcel. Indeed this idea is of supreme importance in his dramas, and it is expressed as in Ibsen's plays through real characters. We know from Marcel's later plays that he, like Ibsen, needed only a chance word or a chance meeting to fire his imagination to create these characters.

Unlike Ibsen, Marcel did not write social dramas until very recently in his two latest plays; and even these he is loathe to place in such a category.

Though René Lalou in *Le Théâtre en France depuis 1900* says that there is nothing more false than calling Curel the French Ibsen unless it is giving this same title to Gabriel Marcel or to Albert Camus,[1] there seems little doubt that Marcel is influenced by Curel, as well as by Ibsen. In his first published play *La Grâce*, Marcel poses, though in quite a different manner, the same problem dealt with in Curel's *La Nouvelle Idole*, the conflict between religion and science. In *La Nouvelle Idole* a child, because of her religious faith, sacrifices herself for science. The man of science learns that above and beyond scientific laws there is another law, the law of God. He discovers that the child's faith in God is equal to his own faith in science; and the implication is that he dies a believer. This is somewhat the type of "tour de force" used frequently by Marcel. In Curel's play however there is an elevation and exaltation lacking in Marcel's somewhat bitter play.

Another striking comparison can be made of a play of Curel's with one of Marcel's. In 1918 *La Comédie du génie* by Curel was produced. In it, the hero, Felix, an artist who sacrifices everything and everyone including himself in the effort to become immortal, is like Daniel in Marcel's *Le Coeur des autres*. In Curel's play there is also a son, but this boy is able to realize all of the ambitions which his father failed to achieve.

But more important than any similarity of plot is the fact that in the plays of Ibsen, Curel and Marcel, the authors have effaced themselves deliberately. There are no exquisite sonorities, cadences or ornaments inserted for themselves, and the plot is almost entirely an inner action. The portrayal is eloquent and concise and there is never any false note attributable to declamation. The characters express themselves in terms which the precise moment demands.

It is true that Marcel's plays accent man's despair and isolation and misery more than do those of his predecessors.

The relationship of one writer to another is a tenuous one. Every human being is affected by his heritage and by his environment. Gabriel Marcel, avid reader from early youth, accutely sensitive, conscious of and receptive to all currents in literature which flowed about him, long-time critic of drama, could not escape being somewhat influenced by his contemporaries. When we endeavor to place him among the dramatists of the period it is necessary to state what seem to be his own outstanding characteristics.

In Marcel's search for truth he usually discovers a point at which there is a meeting of the things which his characters *do*, with the things which they *are*. Here the characters and not the author seek to reveal themselves.

Perhaps the outstanding and defining quality of Marcel's plays—that quality which distinguishes him from his predecessors and his contemporaries—is his insistence on depicting the tragedy of human beings, tortured by their powerlessness to understand themselves and by their desperate efforts to solve the question "who am I?"—"Of what value is my life?" It is not strange that we often do not comprehend these people when they themselves do not understand their own motivations. The plays, never developed by exterior events, always having their roots in the subconscious, often find their solution in a mystic transcendentalism. They are written by a thinker who is addressing an audience willing to think and accept the sometimes unpleasant realities of human personality. It also seems necessary at this point to speak of Marcel's comparative lack of success in the theatre. It is a fact that for a long time, he had not won the recognition that his admirers considered his due. Lalou says in *Le Théâtre en France depuis 1900*:

> Cette étude ne serait pas complète si je ne signalais pas une nouvelle conception du drame, défendue récemment par M. Gabriel Marcel. Le drame, tel que le conçoit ce philosophe, ne se pose pas en principe par rapport à la Comédie ou à la Tragédie. Il reste cependant dans la ligne de Drame bourgeois en ce qu'il est une tragédie qui n'ose pas aller jusqu'au bout.
>
> M. Marcel fait admirablement la critique du théâtre à thèses, en indiquant que c'est seulement un théâtre à problème, un problème étant, une opposition de deux données dont la solution peut être trouvée objectivement sans engagement ce celui qui la pose ou qui la résoud—sans engagement par conséquent pour l'auteur, ni pour le spectateur. C'était bien le cas des drames de Dumas fils, et de tout ce théâtre de la sensibilité dont il vient d'être question.
>
> M. Marcel oppose à cette conception celle d'un théâtre de mystère, où le problème posé ne peut l'être sans que l'auteur ni le spectateur ne puisse le poser sans sentir en quelque sorts pris aux entrailles, ni le résoudre sans s'engager personellement dans la solution.
>
> J'ai essayé de montrer que le mouvement d'engagement du spectateur est le mouvement tragique par excellence. Mais M. Marcel veut dépasser la tragédie; il réclame non seulement que l'auteur arrive à provoquer chez ce spectateur la prise de conscience d'une situation, mais encore qu'il lui fasse partager la solution que l'auteur lui-même a vécue. Qui ne voit que la nouvelle formule n'est *qu'une quintessence du théâtre à thèse* auquel elle demeure fidèle quisqu'elle réclame une solution?

C'est en somme, une renaissance, plus subtile, et moralement très émouvante, du théâtre didactique.

In another chapter of Touchard's *Le Théâtre de la sensibilité*, Touchard says that Marcel has vindicated himself of the accusation that his plays are *pièces à thèse* by saying that the spectator must be led by the author to share "le mystère au plus haut degré qui soit conciliable avec les exigences de l'art ..."

Gabriel Marcel, lui aussi, n'aura vraiment touché le grand public que depuis la Libération, bien qu'il ait fait représenter auparavant de nombreux ouvrages; *Le Coeur des autres* (1920), *La Gráce* (1921), *Le Regard neuf* (1922), *La Chapelle ardente* (1925), *Le Dard* (1937), *Le Fanal* (1938). A ses débuts, Gabriel Marcel fut rangé, un peu rapidement, parmi les successeurs d'Ibsen et de Curel. Il dut même soutenir une courtoise controverse avec Pierre-Aimé Touchard qui l'accusait, dans son *Dionysos*, de nous proposer une quintessence du théâtre à thèse ...[2] Mais resterions-nous quelques centaines d'amateurs de telles altitudes à entendre parler les personnages de Gabriel Marcel sur les tréteaux de notre imagination? Nous l'aurions pu craindre, il y a quinze ans. Les représentations d'*Un Homme de Dieu* (1925) et du *Chemin de Crête* (1936) à Paris et à Bruxelles en 1950, ont prouvé que des milliers d'auditeurs avaient compris l'importance d'une oeuvre où sont refusées toutes les parures qui seraient des concessions à une mode éphémère.

Ruth Nanda Anshen in *World Perspectives* says: "The suffering and hope of this century have their origin in the interior drama in which the spirit is thrust as a result of the split within itself, and in the invisible forces which are born in the heart and mind of man ... Man, from the very depth of his soul cries out for the unmediated whole of feeling and thought."[3]

"Feeling and thought," this is the combination out of which springs Marcel's dramatic works; the old formula for the "pièces d'idées" of Ibsen and Curel. But this is our age, and Marcel uses its vocabulary. He recognizes loneliness, suffering and despair in our lives. His characters express these things pitilessly and relentlessly. For Marcel, the man of our century yearns to consecrate himself; and Marcel's characters tell us that this can be accomplished through the deepening of a communion with the universe. This seems the essence of Gabriel Marcel.

Perhaps the most important event in the theatre at the beginning of the Twentieth Century was the appearance of the work of Paul Claudel. In 1886, Claudel was converted to Catholicism. He then began to fulfil what he considered the mission of the poet to try to solve the enigma of the universe, in order to find the image of God. He believed that every living being had an obligation to God, "Chaque homme diffère des autres ... suivant la partie et le moment de la création dont il est appelé à jamais rester dans le regard de Dieu l'oblateur et le témoin".

In Marcel's theatre as in Claudel's, religion plays a fundamental role. Both men, in their search for a solution to the enigma of life, reject the "néant" and find God. Both are dominated by the idea of sacrifice and of death—not the death that brings terror, but the death that brings liberation and hope. Claudel's is a poetic theatre, in which he places his characters solidly on this earth, and develops them against a background of mysticism.

Critics agree in marking the period around 1930 as the end of one era in the French theatre and the beginning of another which has continued up to the present. After 1930 the message of Claudel began to bear fruit. Character was portrayed by many writers, more by intuition than by analysis more by suggestion than by definition. The result was a more poetic theatre.

As we glance at Gabriel Marcel's chief contemporaries, we note first those who follow a poetic or historical pattern—Giraudoux, Anouilh, Cocteau and Montherlant. Marcel's modern characters and realistic situations create a totally different atmosphere from that of the plays of these four men, and certainly the inclusion of Giraudoux and Cocteau could be challenged on the ground that they are too remote from Marcel to concern us here. However there are still certain basic ideas which they share. The fundamental differences however are much more marked.

This poetic theatre, in spite of its handling of basic human problems creates a totally different atmosphere and impression than that which any theatre of ideas could do—and therein lies its chief characteristic quality.

Marcel's characters, though sometime involved in situations and dilemmas that are not commonplace, are always completely plausible and have a life and will of their own apart from their author. This is not true of Giraudoux, who always interposes himself between us and his characters. In an article on *La Folle de Chaillot*, Marcel makes the following comment: "Imaginez un La Fontaine déployant, au théâtre, les dons qui nous émerveillent dans ses fables, et on peut gager que ce La Fontaine dramaturge eût été le précurseur de Giraudoux ... quel que soit son éclat, quelle que soit sa séduction, la faiblesse profonde du théâtre de Giraudoux me paraît consister dans le fait que jamais, ou presque, l'auteur ne s'efface devant ses personnages; il leur impose son langage, sa subtilité, sa préciosité. C'est une raison suffisante pour que ceux-ci soient d'une façon générale, et à très peu d'exceptions près, dépourvus de cette présence qui est le signe authentique de la réussite dramatique."[4]

While recognizing the very real success of *La Folle de Chaillot* and admiring the sorcery of Giraudoux's unpremeditated fantasy, Marcel still sees the dangers of his contemporary's vast prestige:

> On peut craindre que l'influence de Giraudoux dans le domaine du théâtre n'ait été, dans l'ensemble, plutôt fâcheuse. Il n'est pas difficile de comprendre pourquoi: ce qui est transmissible ici, c'est exclusivement le procédé; or, c'est *malgré* le procédé que nous aimons, que nous admirons, que nous avons raison d'aimer et d'admirer Giraudoux, et peut-être le mot "malgré" ne rend-il pas ici exactement ma pensée. Mieux vaudrait dire que nous l'aimons a travers ces procédés, et en un certain sens contre ceux-ci. Mais on peut affirmer qu'il n'y a pas de moyen plus sûr de le trahir que d'imiter ces procédés; même s'il est excessif de les assimiler à des manies ou à des tics, ils ne peuvent, en aucun cas, se laisser dissocier d'un pouvoir magique, mais qui n'est pas lui-même absolument à l'abri des chocs en retour auxquels la sorcellerie expose invariablement ceux qui l'exercent avec le plus de maîtrise. Mais il est évident que ce choc en retour se manifeste à plein et de la façon la plus nocive contre l'apprenti

sorcier auquel la puissance effective a été refusée, et qui, avec maladresse et nervosité, s'évertue à en surprendre les secrets. Il suffit de concentrer son attention sur une oeuvre comme *La Folle de Chaillot* pour reconnaître à quel point ce qui vaut en elle est inimitable.

Anouilh's theatre is as far removed from the tradition of the problem play and the play of ideas, as is that of Giraudoux and Claudel. Though Anouilh is influenced by many, he subscribes to no system, and no one is for him an exclusive master. His theatre resembles that of many writers in some respects; he is nevertheless totally himself. He disdains certain credibility for an unreal verity which is purely poetic in essence. The plays mostly belong in the category of a "divertissement" of the mind or intelligence, but never become truly intellectual. It is in this respect that the fairy-like quality of Anouilh differs from that of Giraudoux which is always intellectual.

It is doubtful whether Anouilh in composing his plays proceeds from any idea. He is a dramatist who demands liberty in all its forms for the expression of his particular type of sarcasm, irony, dream and evasion. But most of all, Anouilh never ceases to take a stand. His theatre is one in which the individual refuses the demands of society, happiness and even of life itself. It is the theatre which in the theological sense is without Grace. This fact, however, is a minor difference between the drama of Anouilh and that of Gabriel Marcel. The great difference lies in the fact that any poetic theatre acts upon the audience in a totally different way from any theatre of ideas and here the comparison of Anouilh's theatre with Marcel's is most striking.

In reviewing *Romeo and Jeannette* Marcel spoke of Anouilh's "parti-pris romantique" adding: "Mais il faut ajouter aussitôt, si l'on veut être équitable, qu'il ne s'agit pas là d'un parti pris littéraire ou esthétique, mais bien plutôt, me semble-t-il, d'un pli authentique de la sensibilité elle-même. Seulement il peut venir un moment où ce pli de la sensibilité risque d'être interprété injustement comme un procédé, et où, par conséquent, l'effet magique, que l'oeuvre dramatique a pour objet propre de susciter, ne se produit plus."[5]

It is as difficult to place Marcel alongside Cocteau as it is for the average critic to find Cocteau's place in the literature of our time. Because Cocteau is a virtuoso and virtuosi will not remain placed, we can only display his chief characteristics in an effort to find some similarities.

Although we think of Cocteau as practicing all the arts, he considers that all art is a form of poetry. Thus he calls his own work "poésie de roman, poésie de théâtre, poésie critique, poésie graphique" and "poésie cinématographique". This poetry he thinks of as a special vision not given to ordinary man, and since the ordinary man is able to grasp that vision only much later, this time difference causes the difficulty in public understanding. Cocteau would be loath to admit that he ever repeats himself but in looking for recurrent themes in his work we find a repetition of the themes of illusion and reality, order and disorder.

Most important for a comparison of Cocteau with Marcel is the use by both men of the theme of death. This is a dominant idea in both theatres. Whereas Marcel believes that life is only a part of reality and that illness and aproaching death bring certain insights, for Cocteau life is illusion and death the only reality; equilibrium can be achieved only by death (*La Machine infernale* and *Les Parents terribles*).

Beyond this, it would be difficult to find any likeness in the theatre of these two dramatists. Whereas Cocteau has always striven both to please and to shock the public and has called upon every extraordinary technical means to accomplish this purpose, including disappearing horses and talking flowers, Marcel has offered only rather stark drama which the public seems reluctant to accept and characters which are often unpleasant.

In writing of Cocteau, Marcel has said:

Il a écrit une pièce humaine, et, au fond, il n'en a écrit qu'une: *Les Parents terribles*. Mais comment ne pas reconnaître que cette pièce constitue, de son point de vue même, une exception déroutante, une anomalie presque injustifiable? Tout le reste de son théâtre, qu'il s'agisse des *Mariés de la Tour Eiffel* ou des *Chevaliers de la Table-Ronde*, d'*Orphée*, de *Renaud et Armide* ou de *L'Aigle à deux têtes*, appartient au domaine de l'expérimentation théâtrale. Mais n'est-ce pas justement cette idée d'expérimentation théâtrale qu'il convient de refuser absolument, tout au moins en ce qui concerne l'auteur dramatique? Pour le metteur en scène, c'est différent; il est tenu d'expérimenter pour pourvoir oeuvrer. Si les conceptions que j'ai présentées ici même sur la finalité de l'oeuvre dramatique ont quelque fondement, il est clair que l'expérimentation dans ce domaine est parfaitement illicite. Je dirai tout à fait en gros qu'on n'expérimente légitimement que sur des choses et non pas sur des êtres.[6]

Cocteau's *Bacchus* presented in 1951 has a religious theme. Cocteau claims that this play honors the church, and certainly the Cardinal's attitude toward the young heretic Hans (Bacchus) is a sympathetic one.

Henry de Montherlant says in the Postface to *Le Maître de Santiago*— "... Il y a dans mon oeuvre, une veine chrétienne et une veine profane (ou pis que profane) que je nourris alternativement, j'allais dire simultanément, comme il est juste, toute chose en ce monde méritant à la fois l'assaut et la défense ..." It should be added that the Christian vein is not an orthodox one, though Montherlant is a fervent Catholic by tradition.

Whereas in his novels Montherlant extols a certain moral attitude and rejects indulgence, his theatre usually presents the two contrasting elements.

It is in their contradictions that Gabriel Marcel and Montherlant can be compared. In each the contradiction is concerned with religion. Montherlant inherited his Catholicism. He has unbounded pride in his Spanish forbears, their traditions and faith, but his spirit of rebellion is obvious in his plays.

Marcel is not a Catholic by inheritance and tradition but by his own choice. In spite of this choice, there exists a conflict in him because of his rejection of orthodoxy and dogmatism. In the discussion of Marcel's plays, many examples of this persisting conflict have been pointed out.

For the most part, the plays of François Mauriac depict a humanity plunged in evil. He portrays passionate human beings capable of wallowing in the darkest crime who nevertheless retain a nostalgia and a thirst for purity. The full gamut of these emotions is best seen in the novels of Mauriac, as for example in *Genitrix*, where a monstrous deformation of maternal love is displayed, or family hatred as in *Le Noeud de vipères*. His plays demonstrate the same vision of a world where evil triumphs although there is also a yearning for a religion of love and pity, and the same qualities which characterize the novels are present in the plays: the provincial background, the evil characters, the frustration of individuals who do not understand their own motivations. Mauriac is concerned in these plays as in his novels with the problem of Grace, and in order to illustrate the saving action of Grace he creates scenes of great intensity, where evil is a reality and yet a mystery.

There are certain similarities between the plays of Mauriac and those of Gabriel Marcel. They both write problem plays. Both usually present man in his less attractive aspects. Both deal with passionate human beings. In both the action of the play is basically psychological. Both seek a supernatural solution for the problems of their characters.

The differences are quite marked however, even though they may be differences in degree only. While in general Marcel's characters show some deviations, they usually can be classified as lying within the realm of what we call normal. With Mauriac this is not true. His characters are mainly people that modern terminology would classify as psychotic. They are dangerous people, capable of any crime; and the deeper they become involved, the stronger becomes the impetus for salvation through religion. Marcel on the other hand does not allow his characters to sink so low. They are tortured because of what they are and because of their inability to comprehend their motives or to communicate with other human beings. They are not criminals, though the result of their acts is often as bad as if they were.

Lenormand's theatre, like Marcel's, is peopled with doubt and anxiety; but unlike Marcel's, it is closed to Grace and Hope. Its atmosphere is one of decadence of the individual and of society. In the individual it is psychological decadence (*Le Mangeur de rêves*) or moral decadence (*Le Lâche* and

Les Ratés.) In these plays there is instability and doubt and compromise with evil, with no ray of hope. Lenormand is a prophet of doom for our civilization, all is catastrophe, evil and death; there is no redemption, no resurrection. Civilization is being destroyed by man's impurity and his inhumanity.

Compared with Lenormand's drama, Marcel's plays appear optimistic, almost deserving the title of a "theatre of hope". Both writers place their characters firmly on this earth, and in both, the characters are passionate and disquieting. Marcel's are an admixture of good and evil, where Lenormand's are pathologically evil. With such characters Lenormand can do nothing less than predict the total destruction of society. Marcel writes of Lenormand, after praising him for his concern with the human condition: "Mais celui-ci a trop souvent subi la fascination des thèses freudiennes."

Gabriel Marcel shares with Denys Amiel, Jean Jacques Bernard and Charles Vildrac in contributing to the tendency known in the theatre as "the drama of the unexpressed." This is shown in Marcel's case by the fact that the emotions of his complex characters are not analyzed either by their creator or by themselves. We learn to know the people Marcel creates through psychological suggestion, their acts, and the words that they say or even perhaps better, through the thoughts they think but do not speak.

It is interesting to note that Vildrac and Marcel share any sort of drama technique because their plays, superficially considered, appeared to have little relationship. This derives mainly from the fact that their characters are chosen from completely opposite backgrounds. Whereas Marcel's characters are, for the most part, sophisticated intellectuals, Vildrac's characters are simple people. In the plays of both men however, the drama is psychological and the problems which arise are solved or remain unsolved in that other reality called the sub-conscious.

When Jean-Jacques Bernard's *Martine* was produced in 1922, Gaston Baty asked Bernard to write an article for the program. Bernard remarked that the character of Martine who suffered because of love throughout the play, never told anyone about her love or her suffering. Bernard suggested to Baty that he would write an article on the value of silence in the theatre. Thus there appeared in the fifth *Bulletin de la chimère* a short article by Bernard on this subject in which he wrote:

> Le théâtre est, avant tout, l'art de l'inexprimé. C'est moins par les repliques que doivent se révéler les sentiments les plus profonds. Il y a, sous le dialogue entendu, comme un dialogue sous-jacent, qu'il s'agit de rendre sensible.
>
> Aussi le théâtre n'a pas de pire ennemie que la littérature. Elle exprime et dilue ce qu'il ne devrait que suggérer. Le romantisme, dans ce qu'il a eu de moins bon, a porté cet inconvénient a l'extrême.
>
> Un sentiment commenté perd de sa force. La logique du théâtre n'admet pas les sentiments que la situation n'impose pas. Et, si la situation les impose, il n'est pas besoin de les exprimer.
>
> C'est pourquoi un "couplet" en dit toujours moins qu'une réplique en apparence indifférente. Est-ce que nous ne sommes pas plus émus et convaincus des sentiments de Sylvia quand elle murmure: "J'avais grand besoin que ce fût là Dorante," que de ceux de doña Sol quand elle appelle Hernani son "lion superbe et genéréux?"
>
> La langue française a ceci de merveilleux qu'elle s'enrichit en se dépouillant. C'est par là qu'elle se prête admirablement au théâtre. Le mot en soi n'est qu'un faible instrument pour tout ce que nous voudrions exprimer. Il n'a pas plus de valeur qu'une corde de violon au repos. Mais quelles résonances possibles! …

Surely neither Marcel nor Vildrac absorbed the idea of the theatre of the unexpressed as a theory; rather they used it instinctively because of the fact that silence is a permanent element in dramatic art and has always existed in all artistic theatre. Because both men are artists, Vildrac and Marcel found this technique necessary to their artistic expression.

Salacrou, who like Marcel is in the tradition of Ibsen, writes plays which stress the inner or psychological action and the predominance of ideas. He has a horror of rhetoric and didacticism while expressing a conception of man and the human condition. He is a satirist of social prejudice. His plays are concerned with the problems of love and the impossibility of finding true love; but Salacrou's characters, unlike Marcel's, are willing to compromise and to accept their situation. Sometimes this in itself constitutes tragedy. In general, his characters occupy a less favored social position than those of Marcel and they accept their mediocrity without protest.

Marcel's high opinion of Salacrou can be found in his review of *Le Soldat et la sorcière*:

> Il est un des très rares auteurs dramatiques de notre temps à ne pas accepter purement et simplement la condition humaine comme une donnée qu'on ne discute pas. C'est par là qu'il est poète, qu'il est original, qu'il se délivre de l'observation purement réaliste. Je ne pense d'ailleurs pas qu'il ait encore suivi jusqu'au bout ce chemin écarté, aventureux, sur lequel, parmi les contemporains, il est à peu près le seul à s'être engagé ... Jamais il n'est apparu plus clairement que l'auteur dramatique doit, au sens fort de ce mot, être poète; mais jamais on n'a mieux vu, d'un autre côté, que la poésie dont il est question ici est le contraire de la "littérature." Car sa destination propre consiste à créer de l'être et des êtres. C'est à cette création-là que tout doit être subordonné. Le reste est subsidiaire.[7]

And that form of poetry, Marcel claims, is found in *Le Soldat et la sorcière*, which he calls therefore a "Tragédie authentique".

Finally, with Sartre and Camus, Marcel shares certain intellectual dilemmas. The similarities between these two authors are difficult to find, because of entirely different conception of the drama and of the philosophical solutions they propose.

Our particular moment in history created its own literature. Writers engaged in a struggle to seek a new philosophy of life and greater dignity for man.

After the war of 1939, Existentialism began to flourish. In 1946 Sartre published an exposé of his doctrine in his *L'Existentialisme est un humanisme*. He held that the direction of life is not determined in advance; that man does not exist in himself as essence but only by his acts. It is by living and struggling and suffering that man's role begins little by little to be defined. In this search, there is no God to guide the atheistic Existentialist; therefore in searching among the infinite possibilities for choosing his own direction, man is sometimes attacked by "la nausée" which affects him as well as others, because each of his acts serves as an example to others. Man is not alone in the world; there are others making the struggle with him. He occupies a certain position among this group and his liberty consists in choosing a direction toward a certain goal and making the most of the goal he has chosen. The only values which he recognizes are those which he created in relation to his acts, and his only duty is to respect the liberty of others.

The theatre is a means for Sartre to dramatize his philosophic ideas. Despite his undeniable gift for the theatre, his plays are "pièces à thèses" and his characters are not free, living beings but automata destined to be the spokesmen of the author. The plays can be roughly divided into two categories—those which express Sartre's atheism—*Les Mouches, Huis-Clos, Le Diable et le bon Dieu*; and those which deal with politics—*Morts sans sépulture* and *Les Mains sales.*

It is easy to see that any resemblance between the work of Sartre and Marcel is more apparent than real. Though they agree on two major points in Existentialism, e.g., that life on earth seems without direction, in fact absurd, and that man is free to choose his own role in life, Marcel's solution to life's enigma is different as his drama is completely different.

That form of Existentialism called Christian or Catholic Existentialism in France, cannot be attributed entirely to Marcel. One must mention the Germans, Karl Jaspers and Husserl whose Existentialist ideas were formed into a system, as Marcel's never were. The Dane, Kiekegaard, whose faith was Protestantism of the most rigorous type, was the precursor of all Existentialism and a very important influence on any interpreter of this philosophy.

The Catholic doctrine, less pessimistic, preaches that to man who has done the best he can, God will not refuse Grace. But since this Grace is by definition gratuitous, not depending on the merits of man but upon the pleasure of God, this gratuitousness becomes for the atheist Existentialism of Sartre synonymous with the irrational and absurd.

Without attempting any detailed analysis of Catholic Existentialism, it is sufficient here to say that the great

difference between it and the atheist conception is that for
the Catholic, despair is only a passing temptation; that hope
is the essential, and forms the substance of life. Expressed by
Marcel, "je ne suis pas éloigné de croire que l'espérance est à
l'âme ce que la respiration est à l'être vivant".[8]

Most students of Marcel's philosophical works have
sought to find in his theatre not only a link with his ideas but
an actual exteriorization of his philosophical thinking.
Marcel himself has frequently denied that this is in any way
true. He considers his drama a completely separate means of
expression, and a student of this drama as such discovers
that it can and does stand completely on its own. Of course
no expression in art can be separated from its creator; they
are basically one. But it is a false premise to seek in Marcel's
various plays the dramatization of ideas expressed in his
philosophical works. The theatre is Marcel's love and his
inventive genius guards that love from outside suitors, even
those of his own creation (e.g., his philosophy).

In a review of *Morts sans sépulture* and *La Putain
respectueuse* Marcel sees very clearly the virtues and defects
of the dramatist Sartre, who "ballotté entre la dialectique et
l'anecdote", lacks the sense of poetry that would enable him
to escape this opposition that is always fatal in the theatre.
He adds:

> Ce qui me frappe dans *Huis Clos*, c'est que c'est en réalité une
> pièce impasse, une pièce cul-de-sac, qui n'annonce ou ne promet
> absolument rien au delà d'elle-même. D'abord parce que c'est,
> au fond, une sorte de démonstration, ou peut-être plus
> exactement de *monstration* dialectique destinée à imposer à
> l'esprit, dans des conditions extraordinairement artificielles
> d'ailleurs, le type de rapports auquel, aux yeux de l'auteur, se
> réduisent les relations entre personnes. L'*autre* se présente à moi
> exclusivement comme menace (d'aliénation), ou comme ten-
> tation, pour autant que je vise à me l'approprier de quelque
> manière que ce soit. Si l'auteur a situé sa pièce en enfer, cela
> veut dire en langage clair qu'il a délibérément isolé par
> abstraction un certain aspect de la réalité humaine, sur lequel il
> désirait porter la lumière. Il a d'ailleurs été contraint, pour que
> cette sorte d'expérimentation psychologique pût avoir lieu, de
> procéder à une sélection à la fois très soigneuse et très arbitraire.

Ce n'est certes pas un hasard s'il a choisi un déserteur, une lesbienne, etc., et c'est se moquer du monde que de prétendre, avec M. Campbell, qu'il aurait pu tout aussi bien mettre en présence un général, une vertueuse mère de famille et une carmélite. A moins d'user d'artifices qui auraient été instantanément repérés par le spectateur le moins subtil, il lui aurait été impossible d'obtenir la moindre réaction théâtrale en confrontant de semblables personnages, qui auraient été autant de corps chimiquement inertes. Mais, d'autre part, la pièce se trouve n'être possible qu'à des conditions qui la dépouillent du caractère de vérité générale que l'auteur a trop évidemment entendu lui conférer.

Morts sans sépulture et *La Putain respectueuse* me paraissent présenter cet intérêt au moins négatif d'être beaucoup moins tributaires d'une dialectique chère à l'auteur, qui en est cependant moins captif que ne l'est Simone de Beauvoir ... D'un autre côté, je persiste à penser que le thème central de *Morts sans sépulture* n'est pas en soi dépourvu de grandeur. Qu'un chef, qui a la possibilité d'être relâché alors que ses compagnons sont voués à la torture et à la mort, se trouve dans une situation qui lui commande de saisir cette possibilité, parce qu'il est seul à pouvoir prévenir les camarades qui, autrement, tomberaient dans un piège tendu par l'ennemi: c'est là une situation émouvante et neuve et qui me paraît, en un certain sens, beaucoup moins factice que la conjoncture laborieusement réalisée dans *Huis clos*. Mais on peut craindre que l'esprit dans lequel cette donnée a été traitée ne permette pas d'en saisir tout le tragique. A tout le moins, la façon dont l'auteur s'attaque au système nerveux du spectateur, par exemple en faisant étrangler sur la scène le petit François, ne peut pas ne pas porter atteinte à l'élément authentiquement tragique de la pièce.[9]

Like Marcel in all of his work, Albert Camus is concerned with the conflicts between the seeming absurdity of human life and the persistent longing to find a solution. While Camus faces the irrationality boldly, Marcel seeks his solution in another world. Camus' plays—*Caligula, Le Malentendu, L'Etat de siège, Les Justes*, like his novels and essays, deal with the problem of the absurdity of life by remaining sane in the face of insanity. This how Marcel judges *Caligula*:

Parmi les nouveaux auteurs, il convient naturellement de

mentionner d'abord les existentialistes. *Le Malentendu*, de M.
Albert Camus, avait été un demiéchec aux Mathurins. *Caligula*,
au théâtre Hébertot, a été un très gros succès dû, pour une
bonne part, à l'exceptionnelle qualité de l'interprète principal,
M. Gérard Philippe, mais aussi, il faut bien le dire, à une sorte
d'engouement idéologique sans rapport avec les qualités
théâtrales de l'ouvrage. De ces qualités, la principale de
beaucoup me paraît être le style, qui a de la fermeté, de la
vigueur, du mordant. Je crois en revanche qu'on s'est complètement trompé en voyant dans Caligula un caractère susceptible d'être placé à côté de Hamlet ou de Lorenzaccio, par
exemple. C'est là, je pense, être dupe d'un trompe-l'oeil.
Caligula ne nous apporte guère que l'expression, dramatique
seulement en apparence, de la pensée qui s'exprime dans le
Mythe de Sisyphe. Une certaine philosophie de l'absurde nous
est exposée sous forme dialoguée; mais le protagoniste n'a pas
d'*être*, ce n'est pas véritablement quelqu'un ...[10]

Now the question arises, is the "problem play" or the
"play of ideas" still important in an age of great dramatic
vigor and experimentation, or does the "problem play"
belong to the past? The answer seems self-evident. If man is
still important, the so-called problem play, placing man and
his problems in a real world, the world of the present
moment, is of vital importance. However valuable to the
French theatre is the religious nostalgia of Claudel, the
intellectual playfulness of Giraudoux, the poetic satire of
Anouilh and the virtuosity of Cocteau, the theatre of
Mauriac with its pessimism, the nihilism of Lenormand, still
the plays of Gabriel Marcel have much to contribute to the
contemporary theatre. Without the first rate problem play,
the theatre runs the risk of becoming more and more
artificial and less and less human. The theatre needs the
music of Claudel and the ironic smile of Giraudoux, but it
also needs flesh and blood characters in our real world.
Marcel's plays with very real characters situated in a real
world, as he defined them in 1914 in *Le Seuil invisible* deal
with a rather intellectual group of people. But still they are
not abnormal people, such as Mauriac presents; nor are they
psychotic as are Lenormand's; and particularly they are not
mouthpieces of their author as are Sartre's characters.

Though Marcel's characters form a rather special group, they are none the less universal in their needs.

It could be said that Marcel's frequently employed solution by other than worldly means is also a form of escape; but the fact remains that as long as man is portrayed in a non-atheistic world, there will always be a consideration of his attachment to God. If man is not to be left alone in the cosmos, if Marcel cannot thus abandon him, then he must give hope to man in the promise of another world. Thus Marcel's solution is not evasion but the result of a deep conviction of man's relationship to God. This seems to be Marcel's particular contribution to the contemporary theatre.

Limiting himself to modern characters and situations, entirely distinct from Claudel's and Montherlant's historical evocations, Marcel has nevertheless handled the same clash of wills and conflicts of duties, the same themes of renunciation and self-fulfilment as Claudel and Montherlant. With far more subtle characters than the simple folk portrayed by Vildrac and Jean Jacques Bernard, he has like them, admirably suggested the inner tension that only indirectly reaches the level of speech. Through the use of intellectual dilemmas occasioned by a series of unusual circumstances, he frequently recalls Sartre and Camus, though his solutions differ greatly from theirs. He shares Giraudoux' concern with the basic problem of human identity and the inter-relation of creatures without sharing Giraudoux's poetic vision and highly imaged style. Without Lenormand's preference for the unhealthy and the Freudian explanation, and without Anouilh's pessimistic view of the world, he has nevertheless peopled the stage with characters and problems not unlike the ones created by Anouilh, Lenormand and Salacrou. Gabriel Marcel's drama is not an isolated phenomenon; it clearly belongs to the epoch in which it was produced.

NOTES

[1] R. Lalou, *Le Théâtre en France depuis 1900*, p. 84.
[2] Pierre Aimée Touchard, *Dionysos*, 1938, p. 147.
[3] E. Fromm, Preface, *Art of Loving*, p. xiv.
[4] *La Revue Théâtrale*, May-June, 1946.
[5] *La Revue Théâtrale*, January 1947.

[6] *La Revue Théâtrale*, May 1946.
[7] *La Revue Théâtrale*, June 1946.
[8] *Homo Viator*, p. 10.
[9] *La Revue Théâtrale*, January-February 1947.
[10] *La Revue Théâtrale*, September 1946.

Conclusion

Is it true that the public has little interest in an intellectual theatre, in complex characters, in stark drama? Does it desire rather the easy dénouement and immediate solutions? Judging from the small number of Gabriel Marcel's plays produced in France, one may expect an affirmative answer, because intellectuality, complexity, stark drama and no unsolved problems are characteristic of his theatre. Out of his twenty published plays only seven have been produced and these with uneven success. In 1955 when the Comédie Française, on two different occasions, read his two latest plays, the interest was great and the response enthusiastic. But as yet these plays have not been presented on the stage and probably will not be produced. It has been suggested that the public believes, perhaps on account of his philosophical works, that his theatre may be addressed to a selected group. However, Marcel will continue to write plays as long as he writes anything because dramatic expression is his natural medium. In addition to this, his indomitable will, which enables him to disregard physical handicaps, combined with the vigor and richness of his mind and his sense of social obligation, compel him to express in dramatic form the human dilemma as he sees it.

In considering the significance of Marcel's theatre in the light of his experience, we have continually stressed his inner conflict externalized in his characters. We have attempted to show that he wrote these particular plays as a result of his own uncertainty and conflict. This study was necessary as an aid in understanding the plays.

We have learned that for Marcel, the real world, with its insecurities and failures, needs the promise of hope and Grace and an other-worldly solution. But this is only a part

of Marcel's philosophy of life as expressed in his plays.
Liberation comes also to man from a comprehension of his
own motivations. The analytical process that Proust brought
to the novel, Marcel brings to the theatre. His technique of
suggestion rather than definition is an equally effective
instrument in the revelation of motivations.

Marcel shows that the ills which reside in the mind and
soul of the individual are also visible in society. Therefore it
is inevitable that his early plays concerned with individual
problems should have been followed by those which deal
with social problems.

In presenting his characters against their background,
Marcel reveals his greatest strength. His pitiless observation
of his characters, revealing the pretenses and evasions with
which man surrounds himself, brings to the theatre what
psychology and psychiatry have brought to humanity in our
time. Marcel's theatre is a drama of our time, a time of
uncertainty, insecurity and tragedy.

In surveying Marcel's theatre from 1914 to the present in
an effort to choose the best plays, certain ones from each
group stand out. As so-called pure theatre, *La Chapelle
ardente* is the best dramatically, with *Le Coeur des autres,
Un Homme de Dieu, Le Quatuor en fa dièse* following in
that order. In the next group the first choice is *Le Mort de
demain*, then *Le Regard neuf* and *Le Monde cassé*. In the
plays concerned with displaced persons, *Le Signe de la croix*
is undeniably the best, with *Le Dard* second. And of the last
two *Croissez et multipliez* is a far better play than *Mon
Temps n'est pas le vôtre*. Preference is of course a subjective
thing and in all likelihood another student of the plays would
make quite a different choice.

But the ability to paint man and his condition is not
sufficient for the dramatist. The true dramatist must be
master of the means of expression. The theatre must
represent an emotional experience, and the emotional contact between the dramatist and the public may not be limited
to ideas, however true.

The dramatist whose plays are only a demonstration of
man's condition will not stand the test of time. If, however,
he can add to his gifts of observation that mystery and

poetry which disclose the profound longings of the human heart, his plays will live; and it is on this basis that I believe Marcel's theatre has a chance for survival.

Appendix

GABRIEL MARCEL

The Comic Drama

1. *Colombyre* (ou *Le Brasier de la Paix*)
2. *La Double Expertise*
3. *Les Points sur les I*
4. *Le Divertissement posthume*

Between 1923 and 1937, Marcel wrote four plays which were published in a volume in 1947 under the title *Théâtre Comique*. Readers of Marcel's theatre unacquainted with this volume could be expected to find a comic theatre by Gabriel Marcel rather a surprise. Indeed Marcel himself designates only two of the four plays as comedies; the other two plays appear under the title "pièces".

In classifying the plays I should call only one a real comedy—*La Double Expertise*. *Colombyre*, the only three act play, is certainly satire, and, though the characters in *Le Divertissement posthume* perform some strange acts and in some portions the dialogue is amusing, it also is far from being comedy. *Les Points sur les I*, a one-act play, is drama bordering on tragedy.

These plays written simultaneously with the plays discussed in earlier chapters, contain many of the same characteristics as those previously presented, but Marcel by classifying them as comic theatre, considers that they belong in a separate category. *Mon Temps n'est pas le Vôtre* was the first play in which Marcel combined comedy with drama. The quality of the satire in this play resembles the type of satire in *Colombyre*.

Colombyre is the first play in the volume of four, though it was not the first to be written. It was signed by Marcel in 1937 and the action takes place during the summer of that year. The scene is an Alpine village in Switzerland and the characters are people from various European countries who have gathered to protest against a war which they believe to be imminent and to organize "un foyer de la paix." It is a motley group of French, Germans, Hungarians, Austrians, Italians, presided over by a very belligerent Englishwoman, a Mrs. Cliff. It is soon evident that the delegates are here for purposes of their own—not all honorable. There are illicit love affairs, whispers of jail sentences and constant quarrelling among the delegates. The tensions between the various groups are aggravated constantly by Mrs. Cliff and a crisis occurs with the arrival of an old Russian Chtchoubikov who speaks mysteriously of "le grand événement". Some in the group believe he is an agent of the secret police and someone remarks that the man is quite harmless, only very dirty. When one of the Englishmen suggests that he have a bath he replies "Moi un bain? ... un révolutionaire comme moi, je comprends il ne practise pas avec les salles de bains ... du reste ces compromissions avec les salles de bains et autres dispositifs bougeouis, vous pouvez voir où ça a mené mon malheureux pays".[1] He tells them he has been condemned to four hundred and twenty-five years of forced labor when he had not even killed a fly, and that "l'heure est venue de faire honneur à mes condamnations".[2] Some of the group believe he is carrying an explosive in his little bag.

The day after his arrival at Colombyre he is found dead at the bottom of a ravine. It appears that he had had an accident and fallen, but when a large rock is found near the body, murder is suspected. Whether the rock had been thrown on him or had simply fallen when he was passing, is to be determined. Was it an accident or a crime? When the question arises whether or not to call in the police, one of the group remarks that police inquests are always hazardous and that he thinks it best to keep quiet about the whole affair. Mrs. Cliff says she knows only one policeman, the Saint-Esprit, she knows no magistrate on earth only in heaven; besides she now understands why the old man came to Colombyre, he most certainly came to be assassinated. Why try to find the assassin? *"… Je dois avouer pourtant que je ne croyais pas à ce Russe; il manquait trop d'aura pour être un véritable terroriste. It faut dire que mon idéal d'un terroriste, c'est André Malraux; vous connaissez André Malraux?"*[3] Suddenly it is discovered that the cook is missing. He left a note saying that he was warned by his grandfather of a terrible impending disaster.

Now there is great confusion. Everyone prepares to leave Colombyre immediately. They file out and the stage remains empty for a moment. Then come the following stage directions:

La façade du chalet est éclairée par les rayons du soleil couchant. Un jeune Anglais et une jeune Français qui descendent de la montagne en se donnant le bras s'arrêtent, s'accoudent sur la barrière et regardent longuement le chalet.

Le jeune homme.	Quel joli chalet!
La jeune fille.	Si paisible, n'est-ce pas?
Le jeune homme.	Alluring (the young Englishman occasionally breaks into English.) … Quel refuge! Quel asile incomparable!
La jeune fille.	Savez-vous ce que j'imagine, Francis? quelques êtres d'élite de nationalités diverses, venant vivre ici en communauté, à l'abri de toutes les folies qui ravagent le monde—qui sait? travaillant de concert à édifier une cité nouvelle. Harmonieuse. Au service de l'esprit.
Le jeune homme.	Vous avez raison, Suzanne, c'est une pensée qui fait du bien. Il faudra la creuser. Ce chalet, en se réunissant à plusieurs, on pourrait sans doute l'acheter, et si jamais la catastrophe survient … ou même avant, oui, avant qu'elle éclate … pour être sûr … (Ils disparaissent; on entend encore les mots Asile … Refuge … Harmonieux … l'Esprit.)[4]

La scene reste vide quelques instants; soudain une explosion retentit … Rideau.

This is bitter satire. Written when the imminence of World War Two was apparent to every thoughtful person, the idea of a "foyer de la paix" established in good will must have seemed an ironic project.

La Double Expertise, a comedy in one act, written in 1937, is pure comedy. The scene is laid in Paris in an elegant bachelor apartment. The "bachelor" is Gilbert, the divorced husband of Georgette, who, with her new husband, Stani, is visiting Gilbert. The latter has become engaged to a Swiss girl, Hedwige, and has invited his former wife and her husband to come to his apartment to meet the girl. Gilbert is quite nervous at the prospect of another marriage, because after his divorce from Georgette, he had married another girl, Kate, with disastrous results. Hedwige's father owned hotels in Switzerland but sold them all to found a colony of people who do not know any longer how to live or work or love. She tells Gilbert that when they are married he will go with her to the colony and they will lead "une vie végétative comme les plantes". They will watch the cows, and she will read aloud to him—she loves to do it. He will take a nap every day after lunch until three thirty, a very restful life. Gilbert answers in the closing line of the play "Oui, oui … seulement, une vie reposante à ce point-là, j'ai bien peur que ce ne soit encore éreintant …"[5]

This little play could not be less in the usual style of Marcel. It shows his sense of humor and his qualities of observation, his knowledge of human frailty. Here Marcel does not take seriously his characters' frailties, nor suggest any tragedy in the lives of these people who do not appear to take life seriously. He laughs with them, and though the situation and dialogue resemble those in the boulevard theatres, in Marcel's plays there is never a suggestion of vulgarity.

Les Points sur les I. This one-act play, written in Paris in 1936, between November 6th and November 9th, is the third play in the volume of the Théâtre Comique. The plot concerns a *ménage à trois*. Félicie Girondin has consented to have Anatole's Mistress Irma in their home, hoping that he will soon tire of her and give her up.

Irma has brought with her a fourteen year old child by a former marriage—Aimée. The name is ironic because Aimée is neither loved nor wanted by anyone. She has been living with her father who has remarried and now Aimée has been forced to leave. Félicie asks the child if she had been happy living in the Midi, with her father and step-mother.

Félicie.	Chez ton père, là-bas dans le midi, tu n'étais pas tranquille?
Aimée.	Oh! non, pensez ... je dérangeais.
Félicie.	Ta belle-mère n'était pas bonne avec toi?
Aimée.	(effrayée) Qui est-ce qui a dit ça?
Félicie.	Je te demande.[6]

One day, Félicie decides to take her revenge on Irma by telling the child Aimée of her mother's real position in the home.

Félicie.	(se redressant, à Aimée.) Veux-tu courir après ta mère dans l'escalier. Dis-lui que je me charge de te donner toutes les explications. Tu comprends, à toi, toutes les explications ... Ou plutôt, dis-lui simplement: Maman, la cousine Félicie te fait dire qu'elle mettra *les points sur les i.* C'est compris?[7]

Of course Félicie is too kind to carry through her threat and the play closes with the following dialogue.

Félicie.	Si j'avais eu une petite comme toi ... Je ne demandais rien d'extraordinaire ... Le peu que j'avais, j'ai voulu le garder. Le peu que j'avais ...
Aimée.	Ceux qui vous ont fait du mal, ma cousine, est-ce que? ... (Félicie hoche la tête comme pour faire comprendre qu'elle ne peut pas répondre.) Ça ne me regarde pas? (Nouveau hochement de tête.) Je ne le saurai jamais? (Encore un hochement de tête.) J'ai peut-etre deviné, vous savez.
Félicie.	Non.
Aimée.	Vous ne voulez pas que je devine?
Félicie.	Je ne veux pas, je ne veux plus.
Aimée.	Vous pleurez maintenant comme un enfant ... comme un petit enfant, ma cousine. (Elle

tombe à genoux: elle met ses bras autour du cou de Félicie.)[8]

This play is an extraordinarily moving one. It is strange that it should have been included among the comic plays. In spite of some humorous dialogue, the important characters Aimée and Félicie, are tragic figures. The child Aimée is very appealing and the play leaves an impression of wholeness, remarkable in a one-act play. In fact this is the play of these four which contains most of the characteristics of Marcel's serious plays, notably *Le Coeur des autres*. Little Félicie is really a sister of the boy Jean in that play, and Anatole is not very far removed from the playwright Daniel.

Within the limited scope of one act, the complex relationships, inner tensions and tragedy are all implied in the rather innocuous dialogue. This play should be included among Marcel's serious plays.

Le Divertissement posthume. The final play in the volume is in two acts with a prologue and an epilogue. It takes place in a clinic in the environs of Lausanne in 1923, the year it was written. In the prologue, we meet Fauconneau, a former Inspector of Finance and Carteron, old and quite ill. Both are patients at the clinic.

Fauconneau's particular psychosis is choosing telephone numbers at random and speaking to the person on the other end as though he knows that person, sometimes disguising his voice like a woman's.

Carteron, who has been a patient at the sanatorium on many previous occasions, realizes the state of his own health and speaks frequently of death. He tells Fauconneau:

… Le monde où nous vivons me fait l'effet d'être agencé. Vous ne croyez pas? J'ai l'impression que … derrière la scène … il y a des coulisses, des couloirs tout au moins … et puis, enfin, après le baisser du rideau, on a bien le droit d'espérer … un rappel. Just le temps de jeter un petit coup d'oeil.[9]

Carteron is planning an "amusing" plot against his heirs, a nephew, Emile Favier, his wife Louise, and their daughter Suzanne. Favier is a professor at the university. He loves his profession and everyone in the town of Breuil is his friend.

When Louise emphasizes this fact to Carteron by saying "à Breuil nous ne comptons que des amis", Carteron answers "que des amis",[10] the intonation of his voice shows that he is following a train of thought. Fauconneau watches him. Louise adds that Emile hasn't a single enemy; he doesn't concern himself with politics. Carteron answers "Bravo! Et puis il faut dire une chose, c'est que si jamais vous aviez des ennemis, il est probable que vous ne le sauriez pas."[11]

Carteron has begun to plan his little joke. And when the Favier family leaves the clinic he goes to his desk and begins to write. "Mes chers enfants", on le voit chercher ses mots … son corps tout entier est secoué par une sorte de frisson).

Fauconneau.	"Qu'est-ce que vous faites?"
Carteron.	(avec un cri strident). "Vous ne voyez donc pas? c'est moi maintenant qui vais m'amuser … c'est moi qui téléphone!"[12]

This ends the prologue. Act One takes place a year later at Breuil-sur-Seine in the Favier residence. Carteron has died and the family has just received a posthumous letter. In this letter Carteron tells the Faviers that he feels it necessary, because they were so innocent as to believe that they had only friends in Breuil, to tell them that there were infamous rumors being spread about them all over their town. Of course, there is no truth in this statement made by a diabolical old man who resents his approaching death and wishes to take out his fear and hate upon his heirs.

The results are appalling. Every person in the town, servants, colleagues are suspected and before very long the family begins to suspect one another.

Because of his supersensitive state, Favier becomes defensive and antagonizes everyone. In a very short time all friends have really become enemies and the daughter's engagement is broken.

The climax comes when an innocent remark gives Favier the idea that Louis, his wife has been unfaithful—and he even suspects that Suzanne is not his child. Louise in desperation and anger and wishing to hurt him says that he is quite right in his suspicions, though of course this is completely untrue.

The epilogue is the scene of a seance in which the medium is the directress of a third class pension in Neuilly. The Faviers, having found Breuil impossible to live in any longer, have taken up residence there.

Out of the darkness in the room the voice of Carteron is heard saying "Assez! Assez! ... Je vous dis que j'en ai assez ... ca ne m'amuse plus ... ce n'est plus drôle du tout ... je veux que ça finisse ... je veux leur dire ..."[13] The voice calls for Fauconneau. Louise remembers having met Fauconneau the day the family visited the sanatorium and goes to the telephone, finds his name in the book and speaks to him.

Louise.	... Monsieur, je vous téléphone ... Madame Favier, du Family-House, 118, rue Léon-Benoît, à Neuilly ... Mais si, Monsieur, à la clinique du Val Fleury ... mon oncle Carteron ... nous a présentés ... comme dans cauchemar, a comme dans araucaria, r comme dans ... C'est cela ... Oui, Monsier, des éclaircissements ... Nous sommes plus que tourmentés ... à la suite d'une lettre ... d'une lettre (Favier la tire par derrière et l'oblige à lâcher le récepteur.) Mais tu es fou, Emile![14]

Fauconneau arrives at the pension in his pajamas a short time after. Favier and Louise question him regarding the letter. He tells them that he did not know the contents of it but that he had reason to believe it to be "une mystification".

While Fauconneau is speaking, the voice of Carteron is heard again.

La voix de Carteron.	(gémissante.) Pas pu ... pas réussi ...
L'autre voix.	Va! ne te frappe pas ... Ils finiront bien par dégotter.
Une voix scandalisée.	Oh! Oh! quel affreux langage!
L'autre voix.	La vérité qu'ils méritent!
Un écho que emplit la salle.	La vérité qu'ils méritent ...[15]

Bibliography

WORKS by GABRIEL MARCEL

Plays

Le Seuil invisible: La Grâce; Le Palais de sable, Grasset, 1914.
Le Coeur des autres, Grasset, 1921.
L'Iconoclaste, Stock, 1923.
Un Homme de Dieu, Grasset, 1925.
Trois pièces: Le Regard neuf; Le Mort de demain; La Chapelle ardente, Plon, 1931.
Le Quatuor en fa dièse, Plon, 1929.
Le Chemin de Crête, Grasset, 1936.
Le Dard, Plon, 1936.
Le Fanal, Stock, 1936.
Le Monde cassé, Desclée de Brouwer, 1938.
Les Coeurs avides, Desclée de Brouwer, 1938.
L'Horizon, Les Etudiants de France, 1945.
Théâtre comique: Colombyre; La Double Expertise; Les Points sur les i; Le Divertissement posthume, Albin Michel, 1947.
Vers un autre royaume: L'Emissaire; Le Signe de la croix, Plon, 1949.
Rome n'est plus dans Rome, La Table ronde, 1951.
Mon Temps n'est pas le vôtre, Plon, 1955.
Croissez et multipliez, Plon, 1956.

Philosophy

Journal métaphysique, Gallimard, 1927.
Etre et avoir, Aubier, 1934.
Mystère de l'être, 2 vol., Aubier, 1950.
Homo Viator, Aubier, 1946.
Du Refus à l'invocation, Gallimard, 1940.
Les Hommes contre l'humain, Ed. de la Colombe, 1951.
Positions et approches concrètes du mystère ontologique, Vrin,
Le Déclin de la sagesse, Plon, 1952.

L'Homme problématique, Aubier,

Books on the Theatre

Bellesort, André, *Le Plaisir du théâtre*, Perrin,
Chenu, Joseph, *Le Théâtre de Gabriel Marcel et sa signification métaphysique*, Aubier,
Doisy, Marcel, *Le Théâtre français contemporain*,
Lalou, René, *Le Théâtre en France depuis 1900*, Les Presses Universitaires, 1951.
Mortier, *Quinze ans de théâtre, 1917-1932*,
Touchard, Pierre Aimé, *Dionysos*, 1938.

Articles by Gabriel Marcel and Others

Marcel, Gabriel, "Regard en arrière", essay in a symposium edited by Etienne Gilson, *L'Existentialisme Chrétien*, Plon, 1947.
——, "Drama of the Soul in Exile" (lecture given at the Institut Français in London), London, Secker and Warburg, 1952.
——, Remarks concerning *Le Chemin de Crête* in *La Revue théâtrale*, October-November 1946.
——, Review of *Les Nuits de la colère* in *La Revue théâtrale*, February 1947.
Barjon, Louis, *Un Homme de Dieu, Etudes*, September 1949.
Bernard, Jean-Jacques, *Bulletin de la chimère*, No. 5,
Bidou, Henri, "*Le Fanal*", *Marianne*, May 4, 1938.
Estang, Luc, *Le Figaro littéraire*, December 17, 1949.
Gandon, Yves, *Un Homme de Dieu, Illustration*, June 11, 1949.
Jaloux, Edmond, *Les Nouvelles Littéraires*, January 9, 1937; January 16, 1937.
Kemp, Robert, *Rome n'est plus dans Rome, Théâtre de France*, 1951.
Lalou, René, *Un Homme de Dieu, Théâtre de France*, 1951.
Lemarchand, Jacques, *Rome n'est plus dans Rome, Le Figaro littéraire*, April 21, 1951.
Martin du Gard, Maurice, *Le Regard neuf; Le Mort de demain; La Chapelle ardente, Les Nouvelles littéraires*, April 23, 1932.
——, *Le Chemin de Crête, La Revue théâtrale*, October-November 1946.

This is the end of the play and the one fact that is clear about it is that it is not a comedy. When Marcel wrote it, he was still interested in spiritualism. This play seems to indicate his rejection of experimentation. The following dialogue between two boarders who were attending the seance is interesting in this connection.

Montchabert.	(venant se placer contre la rampe, face au public.) ... Ce n'est pas plus malin que ça. Maintenant si vous venez me raconter qu'il y a là des gens qui nous regardent, qui nous entendent, qui savent ce que nous pensons, mais que nous ne voyons pas ... Eh bien, je vous répondrai que vous être mûrs pour Charenton.
Pokrovski.	... Nous sommes sur un théâtre, nous jouons devant un auditoire invisible.
Louise.	Qu'est-ce que nous attendons?
Pokrovski.	Toute la tragédie humaine.[16]

This play is extremely bitter, showing how utterly baseless rumors can destroy lives. Not one ray of hope breaks through its cynicism. It has none of the quality of tragedy of the preceding one-act play, *Les Points sur les I. Colombyre* also is devoid of any exalting quality but this is satire rather than complete disintegration. Hence *La Double Expertise* is the sole comedy, providing, of course, that one feels that multiple divorce and marriage is amusing. There is certainly much humor in the dialogue of each of the plays, and many of the characters are amusing; but these are not comedies in the generally accepted sense.

It has been suggested that the difference between these plays on the one hand, and Marcel's serious work on the other, is more apparent than real. It is true that some traits of the serious plays are here: weak men and strong women in complex relationships which are revealed only in the dialogue. Inner meanings are never described, always implied. It is doubtful however that Le Théâtre Comique adds any considerable stature to the dramatic work of Gabriel Marcel.

NOTES

1 *Colombyre*, p. 92.
2 *Ibid.*, p. 93.
3 *Ibid.*, p. 133.
4 *Ibid.*, p. 153.
5 *La Double Expertise*, p. 184.
6 *Les Points sur les I*, p. 216.
7 *Ibid.*, p. 216.
8 *Ibid.*, p. 224.
9 *Le Divertissement posthume*, p. 241.
10 *Ibid.*, p. 245.
11 *Ibid.*, p. 255.
12 *Ibid.*, p. 255.
13 *Ibid.*, p. 343.
14 *Ibid.*
15 *Ibid.*, p. 355.
16 *Ibid.*, pp. 346–47.